STAGE DESIGN

A Practical Guide

Gary Thorne

Foreword by Tanya Moiseiwitsch

The Crowood Press

First published in 1999 by
The Crowood Press Ltd
Ramsbury, Marlborough
Wiltshire SN8 2HR

www.crowood.com

This impression 2005

© Gary Thorne 1999

All rights reserved. No part of this publication may
be reproduced or transmitted in any form or by
any means,electronic or mechanical, including
photocopy, recording, or any information storage
and retrieval system, without permission in
writing from the publishers.

**British Library Cataloguing-in-Publication
Data**
A catalogue record for this book is available from
the British Library.

ISBN 1 86126 257 4

Dedication

To Gordon and Peggy in love and
gratitude for a lifetime of
encouragement.

Motley in honour of a course of study.

Charles Russell with respect for
tremendous support.

Reprint Acknowledgements
Pages 84–6 © 1977, 1979 Tennessee Williams.
Reprinted with permission of the University of the
South, Tennessee.
Pages 89–90 © 1974 Alan Ayckbourn. Reprinted
with permission of Chatto & Windus.
Page 90 © 1979 Bill Owen. Reprinted with
permission of Samuel French.
Page 92 © 1970 George Furth, Stephen
Sondheim, Hal Prince. Reprinted with permission
of William Morris Agency Inc., NYC.
Page 94 *A Doll's House*, Henrik Ibsen. Translated
by Peter Watts (Penguin Classics, 1965). © Peter
Watts, 1965. Reprinted with permission of
Penguin UK.
Page 96 © 1983 Richard O'Brien. Reprinted with
permission of Richard O'Brien.

Cover Credit:
Zastrozzi at Alberta Theatre Projects,
Director: Bob White
Photographer: Trudie Lee

Typefaces used: Photina (*headings and text*),
Book Antiqua (*boxed matter*)

Typeset and designed by
D & N Publishing
Membury Business Park
Lambourn Woodlands
Hungerford, Berkshire.

Printed and bound by Arrowsmith, Bristol.

CONTENTS

FOREWORD

By Tanya Moiseiwitsch

My enthusiasm for writing this Foreword comes with having had a very full and exciting life in the theatre as a designer. In particular, designing with director Sir Tyrone Guthrie created opportunities which I think were so fortunate. I shared with Guthrie his belief in the collaborative aspects of theatre, for the ensemble of actors and community of technicians, artists and crafts people. From the architect through to the shoe maker, each shares a valued part of the whole whose focus is on actors and their relationship with an audience. My rewards come from a wide diversity of design spanning many years and include the pleasure of guidance and assistance through sharing responsibility with directors and the team.

The arena or open stage demands an economy of design. Striving for the essential meant keeping a sense of proportion. Through trial and error, patience and a critical eye, design is pared down to clarify. A guiding belief in 'less is more' prevailed, with neither too little atmosphere to lose effect nor an excess to overwhelm. Innovation and a unified, distinct visual style of design supports the actor.

To design, one needs to develop interpretative skills, to effectively follow a director's point of view. What the director aims at needs to be understood and carefully considered. For all those involved, the collective aim is to support the play. The opening night is such a relief to the designer, it enables you really to enjoy the play. Theatre is ephemeral and the memory of the event is what one has to go on.

I have a memorable, great favourite of a performance which was on the open thrust stage of the Tom Patterson at the Stratford Festival in 1990, a shoe-string production called *The Knight of the Burning Pestle* directed by

Bernard Hopkins and designed by Gary Thorne. A charming show with many innovative touches, the ensemble were in part senior members of the acting company together with the Young Company. It was on the opening night that a working friendship with Gary began which is still enjoyed today.

ACKNOWLEDGEMENTS

Grateful thanks to the Wardrobe, Carpentry, Property and Scenic Artist workshops, Production Management and Stage Management for each production herein represented. Their expertise has made possible this book.

With special thanks to each theatre company and the following individuals: Neil Fraser (Head of Lighting Design), Royal Academy of Dramatic Art, London; Peter Dean (Deputy Director of Technical Theatre) and Clive Timms (Head of Opera Studies), The Guildhall School of Music and Drama, London, *Albert Herring* 1998 Director Thomas de Mallet Burgess, Lighting Kevin Sleep, Photography Roger Howard; Sebastian Hall and Staff at Polka Theatre for Children, *A Patchwork Quilt* Director Michael Miller, Lighting Neil Fraser, *Starlight Cloak* Director Vicky Ireland, Lighting Neil Fraser, *Beowulf* Director Roman Stefanski, Lighting Neil Fraser, *Wizard of Oz* Director Roman Stefanski, Photography Roger Howard; Pop-Up Theatre, London, Michael Dalton, Jackie Eley, Jane Wolfson, Penny Bernand, *Boogie Woogie Bug Band, Pop in a Box, Spilt Milk, Cuckoo Time, Marjorie Daw*; Arts Educational Drama School, London, *House of Blue Leaves, Vieux Carré, The Linden Tree, Blood Wedding, The Matchgirls*, Directors David Robson, Adrian James, John Perry, Ian Goode, Lighting Di Stedman; The Lyric Theatre London and Pop-Up Theatre, *Hansel and Gretel* Director Jonathan Holloway, Lighting Ace McCarron; Alberta Theatre Projects Canada, *Lettice and Lovage* Director D. Michael Dobbin, Lighting Linda Babins, *Zastrozzi* Director Bob White, Lighting Harry Frehner, *Search for Signs of Intelligent Life in the Universe* Director David Latham, Lighting Brian Pincott, *Six Degrees of Separation* Director Bob White, Lighting Brian Pincott, *Hunter of Peace* Director D. Michael Dobbin, Lighting Harry Frehner, *Johannesburg* Director Ronalda Jones, Lighting Harry Frehner, *Tuck Tuck* Director Bob White, Lighting Harry Frehner, *All Fall Down* Director Mary Vingoe, Lighting Harry Frehner, all photography Trudie Lee; Mercury

ACKNOWLEDGEMENTS

Theatre Colchester, *Murder in the Cathedral* Director Zoe Hicks, Lighting Jim Bowman; Stratford Festival Canada 1988–1993, *The Knight of the Burning Pestle* Director Bernard Hopkins, Lighting Kevin Fraser, *Twelfth Night* Director Bernard Hopkins, Lighting Harry Frehner, *Entertaining Mr Sloane* Director David William, Lighting John Munro, *The Importance of Being Earnest* Director David William, Lighting John Munro, *Love for Love* Designers Stephanie Howard and Ann Curtis, *Three Sisters and The Shoemaker's Holiday* Designer Debra Hanson, *Comedy of Errors* Designer Patrick Clark, *Kiss me Kate* Designer Brian Jackson, Photography Terry Manzo, David Cooper, Andy Foster; The Grand Theatre London, Canada, *Dial M for Murder* Director Derek Goldby; JCT Productions, *Operation KRT* Director James Tillett; Banff Opera Centre Canada, *Albert Herring* Director Colin Graham, Designer Neil Peter Jampolis, Design Intern 1988 Gary Thorne; Forest Forge Theatre Company, *The Nightingale* Director Karl Hibbert.

Special thanks to Tanya Moiseiwitsch, Percy Harris of Motley Theatre Design Course, Bryan Lewin, Alison Chitty and David Montgomery Design Studios, David Neat, Atlanta Duffy, Michael Jennings, Annie James, Leni Hall, Annetta Broughton, Ruth Finn, Simon Doe, Lucy Ackland, Zoe Buser, Bianco Mesko, Tara Saunders, Tessa Scott, Saskia Monty, Rachel Postlethwaite, Keith Baker, Louisa Mansfield, Ylva Grefberg, Tara Baum, Rachel Schwartz, Christine Bradnum, Elena Toumassova, Moe Casey, Andrew Burke, Emma Dowden, Rachel Mellors of CeL, and the participants of 'Design an Opera Project' Blackheath Community Opera; at Guildhall School of Music and Drama, Conor McGivern, PJ Booth, Sue Thornton, Soozie Copley, John Philips, Sharon Fergus, Alex Madden, Duncan Clark, Andy Wilson, Sue Hudson, Susan Hooper, Philip Owens, Anna Graf, Bela Romer, Jude Boutland, Michael Rothwell, Graham Parker, Maxine Foo, Michael Shaw, Adrian Croton, Simon Pugsley, Gui Mendonca, Stuart Tucker, Anna Barnett, Sophie Leach, Jo Dench, Cally Mansfield, Steven Smith, Richard Johnson; Jane Riches of 'Art in Architecture' University of East London.

1

INTRODUCTION

The audience arrives and prepares to take their seats for the evening performance. Unintentionally and most naturally they bring along with them the day's ups and downs. They have come for drama that most notably concerns action and exercises communication. Perception is through the mind of the viewer. There are codes of social behaviour applied to this experience, especially with respect to the audience. What happens on stage, however, is very much a different matter.

Story-telling takes on many forms. It is affected by tradition and culture, but more by language. The act of performing may be scripted, improvised or experimental. The play's language may well challenge an audience.

The experience is shared, it is a social event – a gathering of groups or individuals from society. On-stage the actors, dancers, singers or performers are illusions of characters from the writer's mind. The convention presents a context for portraying relationships of people in society who have something to say. Represented are collaboration and teamwork, trust and respect, managerial and organizational structuring, leadership and direction, decision-making, aesthetics, values, beliefs, opinion, principles and ethics. The experience reflects commitment. That which is presented has been structured through a process. All aspects and effects will have been exercised, shaped, moulded and constructed into a disciplined time frame. This is a 'live' event and with it goes an element of risk. This heightens the level of anticipation and interest. The audience involves itself through application, reaction and reflection.

What draws an audience to a performance? Answers may be as varied as the ideas found to be presented onstage, yet something has been circulating in society and has caught their attention. Perhaps it is as obvious as being part of a festival or celebration. Perhaps the audience has tried to find a play which interests them. For the audience the drama begins long before

Hansel and Gretel *dress rehearsal with actors Alastair Cording and Daniel Harcourt. The flown show cloth with focused lighting creates a cameo scene set centre-stage.* Director: Jonathan Holloway; Lighting: Ace McCarron. Pop-Up Theatre.

(Below) Marjorie Daw, *a small-scale touring set in a neat black-box. Animated set with floor cloth and properties.* Director: Penny Bernand. Pop-Up Theatre.

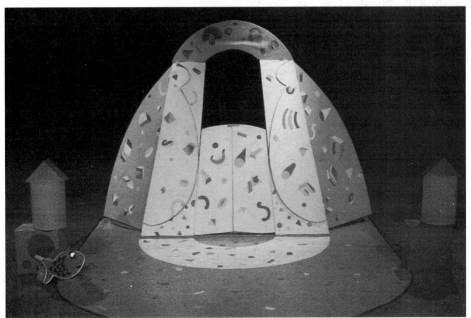

curtain up. Anticipation carries with it expectation, hype, controversy, excitement, intrigue.

As the curtain goes up, so too do all levels of attention. The focus is narrowed down to specifics. What each viewer sees is of particular concern. Being live makes it all the more engaging. The attention is on the acting area, nothing else should distract, or draw attention. The level of attention very much depends on how professional those on-stage and off-stage are at doing their job.

The numbers of people working behind the scenes will vary with theatre type and scale. On the larger scale show planning may go on several years in advance. Smaller venues may schedule plays late on, often making decisions within the season. The play wants selecting so a 'director' will most generally be contracted first. It may well be the director who chooses the play. Directors normally request a 'designer'. However, in repertory there is often a financial advantage in having a resident designer. The director and designer establish aims and intentions. They will consider the more immediate concerns of limitation and constraint imposed by space and budget. 'Publicity' may have already begun marketing images.

Alongside the director and designer at an early stage is the 'production manager' and/or 'technical director'. They handle all matters concerning the organizing and scheduling of technical preparations and production. Most importantly they handle the budget and see to its allocation. A well-experienced production manager familiar with the theatre or space technically is of the greatest asset. Other equally important members of the team are the 'lighting designer', 'sound designer', 'show composer' and 'choreographer'.

Neil Fraser, lighting designer, and designer meeting with a proposed lighting plot. Beowulf. *Polka Theatre.*

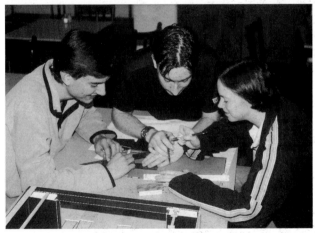

Preliminary production meeting with plans and drawings. Polka Theatre.

(Right) *Lighting design students at RADA working as a team to plot a ground plan from the model box. Peter Harrison, Jon Rouse and Gwen Thomson.*

Throughout the design process, workshops involve themselves by a representative. They offer advice, expertise and opinion. The workshops include: the wardrobe department, and subsidiary departments of the dye room, bijoux or jewellery, decorators, boots and shoes, millinery, the buyers; the wig and make-up department; the carpentry workshop; the property shop; the scenic paint shop.

'Stage management' involve themselves at model presentations to enquire into the 'working' of the show for the rehearsal process and in preparation for on-stage. The 'stage crew' which see to

(Above) *Preliminary model in model box without side masking.* Albert Herring. *Guildhall School of Music and Drama.*

(Below) *A preliminary design rendering with coffee stain.* Operation KRT. *JCT Productions.*

tmotifs.

top different than base.

blue ground

pyremids orange base.

wizard opening red bright. curtain fabric printed glitta texotic.

the running of the show once on-stage consider how trucks, cloths, scenic units and properties might be managed and organized into their on- and off-stage positions. Theatres which have repertory demands, involve masterful juggling acts.

In preparation for production the designer needs to accomplish many tasks. There is the theatre model to build, then the preliminary model or sketch model. An abundance of research and countless drawings and sketches need to be produced. With the finished model go

Property drawings. Starlight Cloak. *Polka Theatre.*

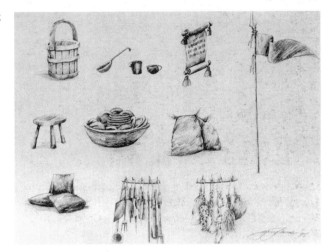

(Below) *Furniture and dressing sketch for an intimate scene.* Zastrozzi. *Alberta Theatre Projects.*

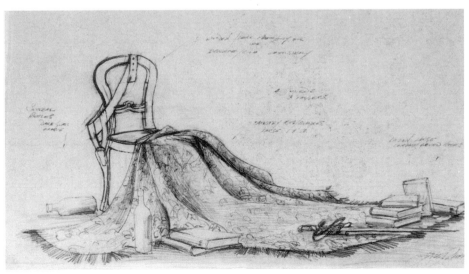

Property maker Annetta Broughton and director Roman Stefanski discussing the animated armature for Beowulf *monster head and hands.* Polka Theatre.

The props department spraying through stencils onto fabric for the costume department. Beowulf.

technical drawings of the detailed set as shown on-stage in section, elevation and on plan. Further technical drawings include the scenic units and all properties and furniture to be built. Costume drawings follow with detailed drawings for wigs, shoes, hats, jewellery and accessories. Copious notes accompany the drawings. Copies of drawings and photographs of the model are distributed to departments. Files or bibles are kept, documenting all material purchased, costs, sources and their in-house treatments.

Production commences often long before actors come to rehearsal. Measurements of actors are taken in advance with fittings often prior to rehearsals. Workshops plot and schedule deadlines particular to the needs of each item. Workshops are more often than not widely spread out making communication difficult.

Each set item passes through stages to its completion. Each step could involve another department. Allowing time in scheduling for this is of critical importance financially. Materials are shopped for well in advance of their being needed. Fabrics for drapery and upholstery need sampling first. They are then subject to being dyed. If samples dye successfully, orders for the full measure of cloth need to be placed and purchased. Order and delivery may involve days, weeks or even longer. Once dyed they may be handed to decorators for hand painting or appliqué. Eventually they arrive in the 'soft properties' department, to be sewn and draped into the design.

The actor's first day is with the commencement of the rehearsal process. It may be the first meeting for the cast and many of the departmental staff. Model and costume drawings are viewed for the first time. From this moment on, the emphasis is on the director, the company of actors, and stage management. Each department makes direct reference to what is accomplished in rehearsal. This process concerns getting the play 'up on its feet'. Stage management schedule and run this period with masterful skill in management and organization, note-taking and communicating with all departments. The director and designer become focused on the actor,

Actors Paul Ryan, Milenka Marosh and Walter James in a rehearsal trial run with skeleton structure and mock-up costume. Beowulf. *Polka Theatre.*

the movement and relationships. Completed set and property constructions will need attention so as to relate to whatever demands are being made upon them in rehearsal. The remaining build requires the same attention. Ideas on paper may need rethinking. For example: a designed property-puppet may have to adapt itself to the abilities of the three performers who manipulate its movement; a throne's cavity beneath the seat may be too small for the actor to hide within, as was originally proposed, in which case the actor may need to visit the workshop for a throne fitting; a sofa may need to be much more solid and securely set, now that it is to withstand an actor's weight as he steps onto the back before leaping over it.

There are new and very real demands throughout the rehearsal period. The designer is often wanted in several places at once. The unexpected always crops up. Initial planning with emphasis on priority-built items and units needs to anticipate all these factors. The closer to being on-stage the more the demands for 'thinking on one's feet'. Being prepared and thorough in design means making a keen and concentrated time investment early on. Production time is never enough. Planning ahead is essential.

The 'get-in' and 'fit-up' on-stage lead through to the various technical

The main stage during a get-in and fit-up weekend. Beowulf. *Polka Theatre.*

Stage management measuring from the ground plan to position scenic elements on-stage. Beowulf. *Polka Theatre.*

(Below) *On-stage set dressing. Designer: Neil Peter Jampolis. Banff Opera, 1988.*

rehearsals involving lighting, sets, properties and costumes. Any 'special effect', costume 'quick-change', set 'scene change', along with every 'lighting cue' and 'sound cue' need working through. They are worked through until perfection is achieved, all timings being recorded and strictly adhered to. Stage-crew and stage management working the show, require precise cues for every action, all of which are practised and plotted. There is a tight time frame for each action on-stage. Safety, however, is never compromised.

The process for design does not stop until the official opening. Decision-making and changes go on until it is right. When masking for off-stage is looking less than ideal then it is a matter to be solved. When objects draw the eye in by being too bright, they go back to either the dye room or props for further breakdown. Low lighting may successfully illuminate a scene yet the aged quality of some set properties may still read as too new. Highlights on a

Highlighting with gold leaf, Ruth Finn uses spray adhesive then brushes on the metallic sheets. Polka Theatre.

(Below) *Louise Poole clearly defined and well located.* Albert Herring. *Director: Thomas de Mallet Burgess; Lighting: Kevin Sleep. Guildhall School of Music and Drama. Photo: Roger Howard.*

carved head may appear with impact to one section of seating, yet not be enough for others. Tightening up the elements to harmonize and unify becomes a major focus for the designer once into the lighting states on-stage. A critical eye is continually required.

The audience will rarely pardon the faults. They remember disasters or incidents that distract from the play and its content. Poor masking that renders visible movement of actors and stage-crew outside the acting area can distract enough to disappoint. A well-presented show is always commented upon and will most likely be remembered. Focus should always be on what is being said, by whom to whom, with clarity of idea communicating itself to all seats. The actor never stands alone.

2

MATERIALS

THE SCRAPBOOK

Commence a scrapbook for the accumulation of cuttings. Begin collecting and assembling images with reference to natural, handmade and manufactured design. Label with name, year, place of origin and source. Create several ongoing scrapbooks. Include photographs, magazine images, newspaper cuttings. Surrounding us daily is a substantial library of free throw-away reference material. Categorize these images under specific titles. Begin with hairstyles, shoes, furniture, foliage and trees, flowers, fencing, ethnic costuming, traditions and rituals, lighting, building materials and so on. Archival scrapbooks become an excellent reference.

SKETCHBOOKS AND PAPER

Hardcover sketchbooks for project work, exercises and as a diary prove ideal. The artist's sketchbook is available in various size formats. Sketchbooks serve many purposes and their portability adds to their practicality. A sketchbook that is smaller than A4 is perhaps more suitable for the pocket, for daily sketching and recording ideas while on the move.

Thoughts are bound together in the hardcover format. The presentation of ideas portray a process in thinking through and discovering. The larger formats encourage a bolder creative approach. Paste, write, sketch, draw and paint into your sketchbook. However, watercolour is best suited to the heavier-weight paper sketchbooks. Build up on the pages imaginative ramblings. Apply the foundations of design. Sketchbooks should exhibit an inquisitive mind, searching and exploring, and be brimming with ideas. Sketchbooks fulfil a purpose.

Sketchbook quality differs so as to serve a purpose. Since paper quality varies significantly with manufacturer and book type, it is important to choose

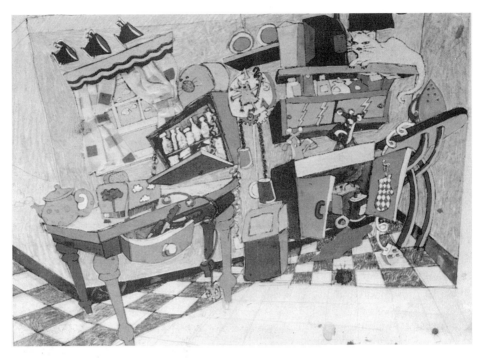

A sketchbook collage for Spilt Milk, *small-scale touring.* Pop-Up Theatre.

something suitable for your intended task. Paper is manufactured in various ways for specific purposes – for example, for drawing, painting, printing or construction. Paper sample packs from specialist art shops offer an introductory range. Keep a record of sample papers, the manufacturer's name, intended use, price, size and surface characteristics.

Sketchbooks

Hardback books, acid-free cartridge paper, for drawing. Gsm 90–140.

Watercolour Sketchbooks

100 per cent cotton rag paper, acid-free, mould-made, HP, NOT or Rough surfaces available. Gsm 140–638.

Paper

The three main surfaces types are: HP, NOT and ROUGH.

HP is the smoothest surface, formed through the manufacturing process. This is through HP or hot pressing. The pressing is done between sheets of metal.

The process of CP or cold pressing is the alternative for smooth surfaces.

NOT is a less smooth surface that has not been pressed by a hot or cold press. Traditionally it has been pressed without using felts.

ROUGH is the least smooth surface. This is achieved by drying the sheets between rough felts, and not through pressing. This paper is generally not handmade. The manufacturing process may vary between firms.

Paper Weight

Traditionally paper weight was for a ream, this being a quantity of paper made to a particular size. This can be misleading in that a large sheet may not be as thick as its ream weight implies. Today, however, the weight is for a square metre single sheet. It is measured in grams and noted as 'Gsm'. Therefore the heavier the paper, the thicker it will be.

You can purchase paper by the sheet, the ream which is a quire of 25 sheets, or by millpack which can vary from fifty to a thousand as the mill prefers. A vast range of machine-made and hand-made papers are available from different countries. *Become familiar with the feel of paper between your fingers.*

Note: h/m is handmade and m/m is machine or mould made.

Sketchbook designs for Marjorie Daw, ***variations on a theme***. *Pop-Up Theatre.*

Cartridge Paper

College cartridge: an economical good drawing paper, with a slight 'tooth' to the surface, which lends itself to charcoal and general drawing purposes. A wood-free paper that comes in natural white. Gsm 115.

Heavy Cartridge Paper: wood-free, matt surface, suitable for drawing. Gsm 130 and heavier weight paper for watercolour and for printing at Gsm 300.

Heavyweight Cartridge Paper: Economical, wood-free, acid-free, with a semi-smooth surface. Ideal for mixed media applications including drawing, ink, wash, printing and painting. Gsm 190.

Watercolour Paper

One hundred per cent cotton rag paper, mould-made with animal gelatine size. Made acid-free. Internally stretched, resulting in a surface resistant to fibre lift, as when removing masking materials. Lines will not feather when pen and ink is used. It will stand up to multiple erasures when using pencil and charcoal. Very stable with little or no distortion when soaking or when applying heavy washes. Often deckle-edged. Available in HP, NOT or ROUGH surfaces. Varies between Gsm 150–640.

Assorted Papers

Pastel Paper: a uniquely surfaced paper for pastel work and printing. When using a pastel paper for watercolour, first stretch it out onto a board with paper tape. Manufactured in a wide range of colours. For drawing use Gsm 95–100 and for watercolour use Gsm 160.

Tissue Paper: available in a good range of colours. Suitable for collage work and scale figure model-making.

Layout Paper: an ideal see-through paper for graphic and design work. Gsm 45 plus.

Marker Paper: extra white non-bleed paper for markers, coated to be streak-free, a see-through paper. Gsm 70.

Tracing Paper: a light- to heavyweight paper for artwork layover. Gsm 60 plus.

Acetate Sheeting: a clear and protective overlay. Permanent markers will dry to streak-free. A specialist acetate sheeting by the roll is suitable for watercolour applications.

Stencil Paper – Oiled Manilla Paper: vegetable-oil treated, water resistant.

Mountboard

Suitable for set model construction. Available in white or with one side coloured or black. Lightweight is 1000 micron or Gsm 725. Heavier is 1500–2200. Use acid-free for picture mounting.

Foam Core or Foamboard: this is a double layer of light white card sandwiched with foam, used as a presentation base or constructed into models giving thickness and structuring. Size 3mm, 5mm and 10mm.

Black Foamboard: is black throughout. Size 5mm.

ART ACCESSORIES

Prepared Size: a gelatine used to reduce the absorbency of paper, boards and lightweight textiles. It is applied with a brush and flows more easily when warmed in a pan of water for a few minutes.

Gesso: a white opaque size, used as a primer for canvas, paper, card and board, or masonry, suitable for oil or acrylic painting. Gesso gives a pure white matt finish with a porous tooth surface. It can be sanded to a glass-like smoothness. Semi-absorbent primers are suitable for canvas oil, acrylic, water and tempera painting. It can be rubbed down with a fine abrasive paper.

Rabbit Skin Glue: a size in crystal form, to be soaked in water and heated through a double boiler. Size is used as a primer for canvas, as a medium for natural pigments. Also suitable for oil paint applications. Size protects the canvas from the oxidizing effects of linseed oil, found in oil paints and grounds.

PIGMENT, PAINT, AND MEDIUM

Pigment

Available in powder form, to which agents are added for binding. Early binding methods involved the use of sizing materials like honey, gum, or egg.

Linseed with pigment produces oil paint. Egg white and yoke with pigment produces tempera. Gums and size mixed produce watercolour. Resin compounds, water and pigment produce acrylic.

Acrylic

Acrylic polymer-based paints for artists have a binding medium of minute solid particles of plastic resin suspended in water. Acrylic paints comes in a rich colour range. They dry rapidly and are water insoluble when dry. They are of a flexible nature and do not yellow with age. The result is a permanent durable plastic paint film. There is a fluid range, made with pigment not dye, offering strong colour with thin consistencies, like indian ink. Disadvantages for rendering and model making could be in their rapid drying time; this does not allow for easy blending and once dry they become insoluble. Brushes must never be left standing for any length of time with paint in the bristle, but must be kept continually wet or rinsed.

Watercolour

Watercolours have a moisturizing agent so, although left standing unused for months, they will immediately dissolve when water is added. The binding agent ensures that the pigment is dispersed evenly. The established names in watercolour manufacturing for artists produce high-quality paints, with an

NOTE

Initially purchase spectrum-coloured hues. For the making of a colour wheel and for your foundation paint-box, choose the pure saturations, or brilliant hues as sold by artist paint manufacturers. (*See* Chapter 4 on 'Colour'.) Buy-in additional colours to the range later, avoiding too elaborate a pre-mixed range of colour. Once you understand the colour wheel, you may prefer to mix, rather than buy-in pre-mixed colours.

excellent range of colours. Binding agents or gums for watercolour may include honey and gum arabic. Watercolour paints contain no opacifiers and are therefore fully transparent. They are supplied in small pans as dried pigment blocks or sold in tubes. A paint box with paint pans becomes a treasured life-long companion.

Gouache

Designer gouache is water-soluble opaque paint that remains soluble when dry. They produce a solid opaque quality and have a good mass tone. The medium is gum arabic – a dextrine solution in water. Gouache dilutes to a wash. Use with sable, bristle or nylon brushes. It is suitable for painting on paper, boards and watercolour blocks, and is supplied in a large range of colours. Excellent paint for all designer tasks from colour sketching and renderings to model painting. Sold in tubes. Note that when the screw tops are left off for extended periods the paint will dry hard, yet remain soluble with water.

OTHER ACCESSORIES

Aquapasto: a gum translucent jelly miscible with water. It adds an impasto effect to watercolour.

Art masking fluid: a rubber latex that, when applied, gives a waterproof film to protect areas from colour applied in broad washes. Removes by rubbing with eraser or peeling. With or without pigment.

Gum Arabic: a natural gum, water, preservative. Increases gloss and transparency. It is the primary watercolour binder.

Watercolour Medium: a pale-coloured gum solution to improve flow of watercolours.

3

FOUNDATIONS OF DESIGN AND DRAWING

FOUNDATIONS OF DESIGN

Design is a form of enquiry. It is an attitude, not a method to be learned and then practised. Design is a plan for order. It concerns itself with form in the most fundamental sense. It is about the markings made by tools, through medium and technique. Design is not an end in itself but more a way of making one more aware. To be effective, design needs to fulfil its purpose. When design is interesting, it then shows individuality. Design's resulting forms and orders are not in themselves an art form.

Design reveals a state that is unique to people, place and time. Design may become dated or redundant yet it may evolve into new forms. The new forms may change to better suit their own time. Practical design needs to develop to meet new demands. Ideas may fundamentally stay the same, yet the form, style and their details may vary. At any given time, one idea may take on various forms between different cultures.

Looking at the invention of tools and materials, we see examples of change through time. Design which falls into categories supporting survival shows a strong sense of ingenuity. Design that excels, does so by being most effective for its own time. Note architectural building materials, household appliances, furniture, clothing, the laser and computer.

Natural design displays: RHYTHM, VARIETY, BALANCE, FORM.

Natural design is represented through: LINE, TEXTURE, COLOUR, VALUE, SHAPE.

Categories of shape are: NATURAL, ABSTRACT, BIOMORPHIC or non-objective, GEOMETRIC.

CHARACTERISTICS OF DESIGN

Line

Mark-making as represented historically exhibits endless variety and ingenuity. Line has reinvented itself with new materials and tools, as seen with the chisel and the laser. Line is a by-product achieved through applying tool to material, be it from the pencil lead on the page, to the formation of lines in the landscape by wind or rain. Line is a series of dots that indicate direction. In a sequence they traverse the surface, either by marking the top tooth surface or by etching themselves into its surface. Mark-making may be permanent or non-durable. A line creates boundaries and will cause separation. All line has character. Line is used both by the plastic arts in sculptural form and the graphic arts for surface type work.

Rolling textured colour effect over a well-textured flat. Scenic artists stand on a bridge elevator. Duncan Clarke, Jo Dench, Sophie Leach, Alex Madden (in hiding). Guildhall School of Music and Drama.

The model for Twelfth Night, *heavily textured with cut-out leaves. The furniture, trap stairwell design and scattered leaves help animate the stage rake.* Director: Bernard Hopkins. Courtesy of Stratford Festival Archive, 1991.

Line obtains style through its references and through adapting itself to suit its function, as well as a type of signature of its artists. Design exhibits a sense of stylish line. The technique employed and how its medium is handled produce a style.

Texture

Line and texture are somewhat inseparable. Texture is automatically created when a line is drawn. It becomes a by-product of the process, therefore unavoidable. Characteristically, it is either rough or smooth. Texture is the tactile, physical nature of line- and mark-making. It is the surface character of substance. Like other elements of design, texture supports idea and intention. Texture is implied by patterns, rhythms, and quality of light and hard pressure on a surface. Texture in drawing is characterized by the volume surface-state, and from the medium and materials used.

Three types of Texture: ACTUAL, SIMU-LATED, INVENTED.

Texture has strong characteristics associated with people, place, object and nature. Texture creates spatial relationships, defines and separates and proposes volume. It can create the illusion of the three-dimensional. Texture adds interest to area, and can be employed to describe the effect of light upon a surface to stimulate tactile responses. A blurring of textural detail may suggest distance, while that which is focused and clearly detailed will seem to advance.

An over-emphasis of textural interest within one area can detract from the appreciation of the whole, thereby destroying unity. Distance and effect need to be considered carefully when creating texture. Overplay may cause spatial discontinuity. This in effect makes texture detach itself from the area where it is presumed to exist. Excessive texture may become no more than visual padding. The pattern may then appear as purely decorative. Texture will enhance the emotional experience. It adds feeling to form, heightening the associative relationships of memory, time and place. Advice is to use texture in careful harmony with other design elements. When used functionally, it speaks volumes.

Sketch model for Beowulf. **The voile flats have texture and pattern drawn onto their surface with coloured felt-tip markers.** *Polka Theatre.*

Exercise

Take rubbings from material and substance. Apply a sheet of lightweight cartridge paper to a surface and rub over with pencil, crayon or pastel to create 'frottage'. Collect samples of frottage in a sketchbook. Create papers with texture by frottage, use as a ground for sketching or painting. Scene renderings and property drawings can be effectively enhanced. Relate texture to the subject matter.

Texture can also be obtained through printing. This is achieved by simple block or stamp printing. Roll out water-based printing inks onto a glass or plastic surface. Take an object or article and press it down firmly onto the rolled ink. Stamp onto the paper surface. Alternatively place the paper over the surface printed with ink and rub with the back of a wooden spoon. Fabric dipped into water-based paints, wrung out and stamp-printed onto paper produces exciting grounds.

Create texture with a spray of paint through objects onto paper. A simple kitchen doily or garden mesh, sprayed through, will produce suggestive textures. The spray also produces a textural quality. In addition, glue down doily scraps to the ground. This produces a spatial interplay.

Use an artist's mouth-sprayer, with water-based washes or inks. Laboratory test tubes work effectively as the vessel for the wash or paint when spraying. Do not

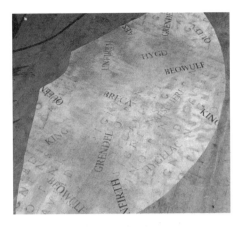

The fabric has texture dye-sponged on before the writing is applied by spraying through stencils. Polka Theatre.

use a mouth-sprayer with any chemically diluted paint, such as those diluted by white spirit or methylated spirit.

Colour

Experiments in colour need to be a first-hand experience. Experiment with colour and use your senses to form an opinion and judgement. Colour theory needs to be learned to be understood. Some artists have a remarkable intuitive relationship with colour mixing. They develop strong feelings for colour. Feelings along with an explorative nature drive their creative work forward. For the student, the purpose of exercise offers up an analysis in colour and its effects. Develop a genuine acquaintance with colour. Colour is very much a matter of direct and immediate perception. The influence and effects of colour are in a stimulation of the senses.

The Use of Colour

1. To give spatial quality to a pictorial field.
2. To create mood and symbolize idea.
3. A vehicle for the expression of personal emotions and feelings.
4. To attract attention as a means of giving organization to composition.
5. To attain aesthetic appeal by a system of ordered colour relationships.
6. To identify by describing the superficial fact of appearance.

Dimensional Effects through Using Colour

1. Contrast of brightness against darkness.
2. Contrast of pure hue against grey colours.
3. Contrast of warm colours against cool colours.
4. Contrast of detail, texture, against planes of flat areas.
5. To imply continuation of design background, seen running behind foreground elements.
6. Use for highlights and for shadow.

Objective Colour: that which is intrinsic or local. The natural colour of an object as seen by the eye.
Subjective Colour: that in relation to the expressive use of colour, without regard to natural appearance. That which is ambiguous, decorative, chosen as invention by designers and artists.
Primary Colours: Those three that can not be broken down to any other hue, the purest form. They diametrically form an equilateral triangle, the fundamental Triad: Yellow, Red, Blue.

To describe any colour tone we have to take account of three qualities: HUE, VALUE, INTENSITY.

Hue

The chromatic quality of a colour, indicated by its name as blue, red, green, yellow-orange and so on. To change the hue of a colour, we need to mix another colour with it. Yellow mixed with orange becomes yellowish-orange, this is a change in hue. On the colour wheel we will represent twelve hues. Limiting the number makes distinguishable the differences. Hue is the pure spectrum colour, at its most brilliant.

Yellow, Yellow-Orange, Orange, Orange-Red, Red, Red-Violet, Violet, Violet-Blue, Blue, Blue-Green, Green, Green-Yellow.

Value

The relation of colour to white and black is indicated by value, and is expressed in terms of light green or dark green. This places the colour in high or low value to its normal spectrum colour. To alter the value we mix in something lighter or darker. We do not change the hue of colour by mixing in white or black, only its value is altered.

Create a chart with black and white at extremes, with seven degrees of value between. The centre value becomes 'middle grey'. Between black and 'middle value' you have 'intermediate dark', on either side you now have 'low dark' and 'high dark'. Between white and 'middle grey' you have 'intermediate light', on either side of this you have 'low light' and 'high light'.

Colour Intensity

The full intensity of a hue is found at its strongest note, saturation or chroma. We differentiate by saying a brilliant red or a dull red. To change the intensity of a hue, we mix in the neutral grey found at the centre of the colour wheel. Neutral grey is achieved through the mixing of two complementary colours. *See* Chapter 4 on the colour wheel and complementary colours.

Make a value chart with neutral grey and a hue at the extremes. Place between them three degrees of change indicating variable intensities of that hue.

The fullness of intensity for any hue can occur at only one value. Yellow when made darker by neutral grey still retains its fullest intensity for yellow at that value. Take two yellows, one at full saturation, and another at the same value but half the intensity. Pass shadow over these two, creating a darkening effect relative to 'intermediate dark'

on the scale of values. The yellow will be less intense for both, yet the one most intense as seen previously in the light will be at its fullest intensity in shadow, with the other remaining half intense as before.

Note that each spectrum hue, all twelve on the wheel, are of differing values, with yellow being the brightest and violet the darkest in the spectrum. Make a colour wheel depicting these twelve hues, and in addition three degrees of intensity created by mixings of neutral grey with each hue. You can now locate the value equal to a different hue. Locate the value of dull yellow that matches in value to spectrum red.

End of Section Exercise

Choose an object from the list below or one of your own. Begin a search on its history and development. Label a scrap-book for this purpose. Look in the encyclopaedia, start with basic knowledge and record everything you find. Collect visual images along with written information.

A list to choose from: books, cooker, cutting tools, car, money, watch, clothing fasteners, hair brushes, dye, entombment, fabric, fans, fireplaces, footwear, gramophone, joinery, letter writing, domestic lighting, luggage, guns, bed or mattress, necktie, overcoat, camera, piano, spectacles, plastics, radio, refrigeration, roofing materials, rope, scaffolding, seating, sewing, shelters, shields, stockings, telephone, transport, vacuum cleaner, water containers, wigs, windows.

Note specific dates related to significant change in design. Research how design in nature may have contributed to its origin or development. Note influences of place, people and culture. Establish its earliest concept and form. Note the functions and purpose, list its inventors. Dates are important. Display

Freehand interpretive drawings of spatial considerations for King Lear.

how it has been used, worn, handled. Record its costs at any time. Add in sketches. Take time and pride in its presentation. Research methodically noting down references by title, author, publisher, date and page number.

Find Answers to the Following Questions:

* What was its original form and how has time changed its shape and why?
* Were any changes seemingly cosmetic or purely decorative and did this fit into historical trends in style?
* How are line, colour and texture an intricate part of its design?
* How does shape relate to its function?
* How have cultures used the same idea and developed it differently?
* What makes it unique to people and place?
* How is today's design a significant improvement?
* What gets in the way of it being a good design and how might it be improved?

DRAWING

Drawing is the initial medium chosen for expressing yourself. Sketching is the easiest of practices and with exercise improves rapidly. The aim is for clarity. Line with character should marry to the idea and intention. Enjoy drawing and take an interest in what you draw. Take your time when drawing. Immediate reactions to drawings generally are that they do not express intentions clearly or accurately enough. Give yourself over to accepting drawing as a process. Do not rush the process; expect it to be involved. Drawing becomes more enjoyable and ultimately more rewarding with more time invested.

Do not try too hard. Straining to draw can be counter-productive. If you find interest in what you are drawing, your involvement will show through. Others will sense your interest, and it will capture their attention.

Drawing exhibits a way of seeing. The result reflects observation and study into a subject or object. The product is a record of an interpretation. Drawing is an enquiry into ideas. These ideas take form and shape. Drawing shows a thinking process and method of enquiry. As a tool it can record, research, reveal, interpret, discover, explore and invent. Drawing teaches, questions, stimulates and expresses. Artists draw using a wide variety of tools, materials and techniques. For the designer, drawing is the most powerful of tools for self-expression.

For theatre the forms of drawing are: architectural representing the theatre space, acting area, scenery; pictorial renderings used to depict artistic impressions of scenes and for storyboarding; costume drawings for characterization and accessories; freehand drawing for furniture, properties and set-dressing details.

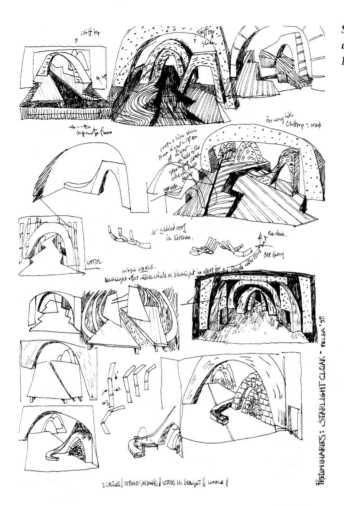

Sketchbook preliminary set design for Starlight Cloak. *Polka Theatre.*

Freehand Drawing
Exercise One

This is an exercise to assist in the development of coordination between the hand and eye. Seat yourself at the table with cartridge paper, size A4 and a soft pencil. Have someone sit directly opposite facing you. Place your pencil tip at the page centre. Look at the face.

This exercise demands that you never look down at the page while drawing. You are about to ask your eye to slowly roam over the face contours and planes. It will be up to your hand to follow this journey of the eye exactly in time with its movement. Where the eye goes, so too does the pencil point. The hand records the journey of the eye. Take it slowly and enjoy the enquiry. Never

Set dressing sketch for Zastrozzi. *Alberta Theatre Projects.*

(Left) *Interpreting the sketched design onto silk with a marker pen.* Beowulf. *Polka Theatre.*

remove the pencil tip from the page. Do not allow your eye to dart about. Explore and roam with your eye across the face, keeping at first to simple observations. Enjoy the journey. Remember, where your eye goes your hand follows. The result is one continuous line drawing. One with a clear beginning and end. Start with a one-minute drawing.

Try again. Each time try to re-look, and record truthfully all that you encounter. If it helps, talk to yourself about the journey as you experience its details. With practice, the record will reveal a remarkable honesty – honesty achieved through simplicity and economy of line.

Apply this same approach to drawing a still-life set-up. Start with objects such as a bottle, book, fruit and vegetable, cup and saucer. As with the face, do not think about perspective. Wander through from part to part as they interrelate to one another. Put this exercise to good use while in a café, restaurant, library; observe people at the bus stop, in front of the television, places where they tend to remain for some time. Draw musicians as they play.

Exercise Two

1. Seat yourself comfortably in a room on your own, with sketchbook and choice of pencils, charcoal, and black and white watercolour washes. First draw a line study as in the previous exercise, without looking at the page. Keep in mind the rhythm of continuous line through the whole room and across all the page. Give equal importance to all, rather than specific emphasis to parts. Aim to capture rhythms that carry and intensify the whole space. Make your drawing enquire into the object relationships found through their spatial positions. Look slowly and carefully.
2. Draw the same scene using charcoal. Concentrate on the values of light and dark form. Give the drawing emphasis in weight. Suggest forms rather than describe them literally. Avoid the particular details and focus on mass and its volume. Use light and dark value to contrast, balance, and create harmony. Try again using values of light and dark in washes of paint.

Work at your drawing to find answers and to solve problems. Note the deficiencies you continually encounter. If your lines appear feeble or uncharacteristic, choose a darker lead or birch charcoal and redraw. Slow down, look harder and aim for a simpler result. If proportions are too distorted, do the drawing again concentrating only on its mass and volume. Simplify form to general shapes.

Let attitude and intention show through the tools and materials used. Let one drawing explore light values, another linear rhythms, another colour sensations, another texture, and so on. Avoid loading a drawing or study with excessive information. Do not crowd out simple, effective ideas. Retain clarity through economy.

Look at how others draw. Note the medium, the tools and surface. What of their intention and resulting achievements? How do they accomplish their aim and through what means? What has made the idea marry with the medium? History reveals a wealth of observation, study, invention and expression in drawing. Visit libraries, galleries and museums.

4

USING COLOUR

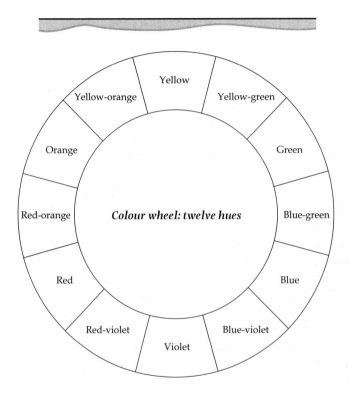

Colour wheel: twelve hues

Yellow
Yellow-orange
Yellow-green
Orange
Green
Red-orange
Blue-green
Red
Blue
Red-violet
Blue-violet
Violet

THE COLOUR WHEEL

It is advisable to draw the wheel as illustrated into your sketchbook using a compass. Follow through by painting onto separate sheets of watercolour paper that, when finished, can be cut and pasted onto the wheel. This allows for experiment off the finished page, with room for trial and error.

Lay out the primary colours; red, yellow, blue. Green may be achieved through mixing yellow and blue to a suitable emerald-green or may be purchased in a spectrum hue. Add in the colours orange and violet, produced by mixing yellow and red, and blue and red. In addition, mixtures are to be made for the intermediates, red-orange, yellow-orange, yellow-green, blue-green, blue-violet and red-violet. The twelve hues are now established.

Notes on Transmitted and Reflected Light

Transmitted light through a leaf shows brilliant colour. Colour may be brilliant through reflected light upon the surface, but colour is more intense when light is transmitted through the object. Almost all materials and substances absorb light. Absorption into the surface texture and material affects the colour which we see as reflected light to the eye. The colour we see comes through both surface absorption and reflected light. White light projected through a prism reveals spectrum colours that unite to form white light. Substances absorb different combinations of these coloured rays. Those that are absorbed are the rays

A false proscenium with transmitted light through the dye-painted canvas. The raked multi-level platforms stand down-stage of a black velour ground-row and flown velour tab. Search for Signs of Intelligent Life in the Universe. *Director: David Latham; Lighting: Brian Pincott. Alberta Theatre Projects. Photo: Trudie Lee.*

NOTES

With opaque watercolours, adding white pigment will raise the value of that colour, making it appear lighter. However with watercolour, thinning the paints on white paper, lightens the value.

Making colour brilliant requires the laying down of neutral grey surrounds. A neutral grey is nearly devoid of colour, and by contrast, the strength of the colour chosen will be heightened.

The degree between light and dark where a colour comes to its full saturation or intensity, is the spectrum value of the hue.

To lighten a blue, violet or purple, through adding white, we weaken it. Yet through mixing in a little complementary, or a little neutral grey (as obtained through mixing complementary colours), or a little of its neighbouring colour on the wheel, the value is changed but not the intensity of the hue.

Bright lights reduce the intensity of colour. By over-saturating a substance with white light, other colour rays or spectrum hues are reflected back to the eye, making less pure the coloured substance.

When light hits obliquely, the reflection increases producing a mirror effect, namely specular reflection. This specular reflection is all spectrum hues together, producing white light. The coloured substance therefore appears white.

In countries of bright light, effects of over-saturation upon opaque brilliant colours, will harmonize or blend colours. This is through reflection of other spectrum hues along with the substance colour being reflected. This diminishes the intensity of colour.

In countries where greyness predominates, opaque brightly coloured substances appear more intense, by contrast with the neutral grey surround.

To the artist and designer, white and black pigment represent the brightest and darkest for that which is light and black in nature. Paper will absorb half the light projected onto its surface, a polished metal surface will reflect all light. Designer limitations are set by the brilliance of white paint to the pitch of black paint. Design hints at nature's true spectrum. Reflected light upon a painted watercolour surface will appear duller or colder than the true brilliance of transmitted light.

that coloured substance lacks in prism colour. The deficiency of the coloured spectrum is absorbed. The rays that are sent back to the eye are those that the substance has in degrees as part of their nature. These rays are the reflected or unabsorbed spectrum colours.

Substances only reflect or transmit colours found in the light rays that are projected upon them. A red fabric will absorb all white light rays except the red rays, therein reflecting them back to the eye. With a light projection containing no red rays, such as blue-green, the cloth will appear grey or black; its surface will also reflect back some of the blue-green as colour. This difference of absorption and reflection of coloured rays enables designers to paint a scene that under light of a certain hue appears in one compositional way, but when light of a different hue is projected, the composition and colour scheme will appear totally different. Brightly coloured substances reflect some degree of their near colour, as a red transmitted will give off some red-orange as well as red-violet.

Yellow and blue are detected by the eye at a wider peripheral degree than green or red. The eye may detect the form and mass of green or red yet the recognition of its colour will arrive to the eye later. This experiment is accomplished through keeping the eye fixed ahead as the colour continues to travel into central vision. Hence yellow and blue signage for drivers on the road. The colours green and orange may at first be perceived as yellow, whereas violet will be perceived initially as blue.

Exercise

Use watercolours for these exercises. Once completed, cut and paste into your sketchbook. Label all colours and their combinations clearly.

1. Produce mingling effects of colour by mixing with black, white and grey. Draw a series of 2-inch squares onto watercolour paper. Brush on water to wet the square. Near the centre add in a hue, while wet add to the surround haphazardly a wash of black indian ink. Let the mingling of hue with black merge freely. Do this with several hues.

2. With one hue dab into a clean damp square in three places, then while wet add dabs of black watercolour paint around these; let them merge and bleed together. When dry, compare the effects of the different blacks.

3. Choose a hue and a mid-grey (between black and white mixings) and repeat the watercolour technique. Do the same for other hues. Compare the same greys with the different hues. How different do they appear?

4. Once the above exercise is dry, choose one sample and apply the same again over the top, using the same hue and grey. This will achieve a layering of surprising tones and textures.

COMPLEMENTARY COLOURS

Use designer's gouache for these exercises.

Complement means that which completes a deficiency. Complementary colours stand opposite one another on the wheel. The complements of red, yellow, blue are respectively green, violet, orange. To test how close you have come to finding the true spectrum complementary of a hue, try the following.

NOTES

Pure saturation or spectrum colours are rarely found in nature.

The neutral grey produced through mixing complementary colours will inherently be an illusive grey. This is never wholly a grey devoid of colour, unlike mixings of black and white. The illusive, shifting quality of neutral grey is never of a flat quality.

Mood and atmosphere through mixing complementary and near-complementary hues are richly varied. Shadow can be effectively suggested by using complementary colourings. The Impressionist painters exhibit such experiment. Black paint creates a dull, gloomy, flat shadow.

Nature's autumn colours are discovered through complementary blendings. Note earth tones in mixtures of red and green, yellow and violet, orange and blue.

ment's complement. The true complementary colour of a given hue when mixed together will produce a neutral grey. If the grey has a bias of colour towards the adjacent colour to the complementary on the wheel, then the complementary is not a true spectrum. By example, spectrum yellow's complementary will be violet. If the neutral grey produced is influenced by blue or red then the violet has too much of its adjacent colour in it.

Exercise

1. Mingle complementary hues. Within two-inch squares on watercolour paper, wet the paper, add in complementary dabs, let merge and dry.
2. Mingle near-complementary hues. For example, violet and yellow-orange. Set these two hues at opposites and add in between three gradations, produced by their mixing.
3. Use the near-complementary hues with white, black and grey to produce pictures or scenes.

Paint out a hue, once dry cut it into a one-inch square. Place this square onto a clean white sheet of paper. Under daylight, stare for a good thirty seconds at this colour. Then immediately remove the colour square and stare at the blank white sheet. After a short time you will see appear an illuminated square, with a colour influence. This after-image is the deficiency of colour rays which go to make white light. The colour image hints at the pig-

Shading and the roundness of surface is emphasized through using adjacent colours to shift the hue. This comes into use on stage with multi-directional lighting tending to flatten out costumes, set and properties. Painting in both shadow and gradation of hue change will emphasize its sculptural

Albert Herring *finished model*. *Guildhall School of Music and Drama.*

form. Fabric folds with painted or dyed recess heightens the three-dimensional qualities. Graded effects with paint create the illusion of real form. Nature under a single directional light source appears very concrete in form.

Creating theatrical illusions to Nature is always a compromise and becomes an art form in its power of deception. Testing material to suit the intention is a prerequisite.

By example take the simple problem of producing black on-stage. Black paint reflects a significant degree of light. Specular light reflected will diminish the intensity and create a surface. Black serge (wool) will absorb a considerable degree of light, yet its surface by nature of the weave will reflect some light. This, however, is considerably darker than paint. Black cotton velour absorbs even more light through its deep pile. There is little reflected light, thus the result is a dense, deep black. The sense of void is emphasized by the diminished surface characteristics.

Avoid the flatness of opaque surface by emphasizing texture and through the mingling of colour. A playful movement on the surface avoids monotony. With monotony comes fatigue. Stimulate the eye and senses by adventurous colour handling, but be careful not to over-stimulate by over-taxing.

5

THEATRE SPACE AND TYPES

Small-scale touring set in a school gymnasium. Strong design to draw the eye to the centre, where double doors open out to reveal another location. Three constructed doorways and four trap windows. Director: James Tillett. JCT Productions.

THEATRE SPACE AND STYLE

Theatres vary in architecture type, technical facility and character. School auditoriums offer different limitations as do

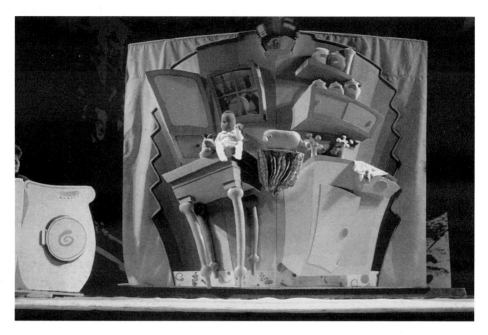

Small-scale touring Spilt Milk **sitting on a theatre main stage, with the evening show set up behind.** *Director: Michael Dalton. Pop-Up Theatre.*

art centres, pub theatres and the village hall stage. Productions that tour will need to consider the technical capabilities and constraints of each theatre, so as to meet their demands. Most theatres offer technical information and drawings, detailing the dimensions and particulars of their facilities. When using an alternative space such as a disused station or warehouse, not originally designed for staging plays, the designer will find on-site research and documentation more complex. This may involve considerable time on location. Familiarizing yourself with a proposed performance space is essential work.

Types of Theatre Space

Arena stage and Amphitheatre; Thrust stage; Proscenium stage; Studio Theatre; Traverse stage; Theatre-in-the-round; Open Air Theatre; the Alternative space.

The Arena and Amphitheatre

The arena is of classical Greek origin. It is an open stage with the audience seated in a fan shape round the performance area. The steep raked seating, once stone steps excavated out of a hillside, stretches about two-thirds of the way round forming a circular area. The steep tiered seating creates an intimacy with good

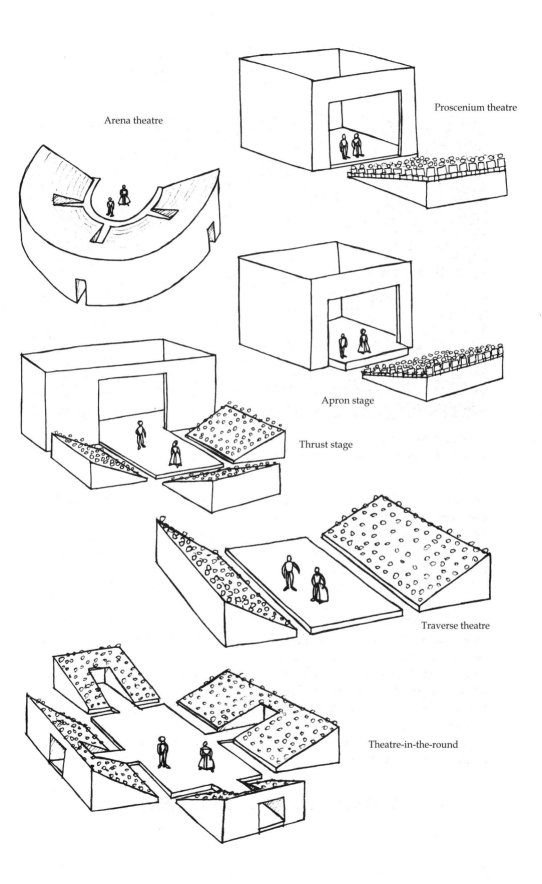

Arena theatre

Proscenium theatre

Apron stage

Thrust stage

Traverse theatre

Theatre-in-the-round

acoustics. Founded traditionally as an out-of-doors theatre, there are examples of this design as an enclosed theatre.

The open-air arena stage requires minimal scenery. Costume design, with properties and furniture feature as essential production elements. The use of variable height platforms may add to the dynamics. The arena may invite imaginative and bold strokes in design. Productions may commence in the evening and feature natural sunset as well as theatre lighting. It is not unusual to see some spectacle in the arena,

Thrust stage with sketch model. The design offers a proscenium, main show drop with door, grotesque and steel mesh wall.
Zastrozzi. *Alberta Theatre Projects.*

such as horses, stage coaches, herds of sheep and elephants, along with monumental scale backdrops.

Theatrical gesture for the actor needs to be of a bold nature. Rapid movements and small gestures with normal conversational dialogue would become lost. Historically this stage circumstance developed a theatrical style which we call 'classic'.

Thrust Stage

England at the time of the Elizabethan period saw theatre move from the established 'inn' or 'yards' to purpose-built, enclosed structures. One Elizabethan London stage has been reconstructed – the 'Globe' Theatre. The cylindrical architecture features galleries or balconies round a platform stage. This platform is set against a back wall, or tiring house with entrances. On ground level in front is the pit.

The modern thrust stage extends itself out into the audience. The seating is positioned on at least two sides. The audience may surround a thrust on three sides. Seating is placed in sections, around the sides of the platform.

The Elizabethan performance was always in daytime. Artificial lighting was not employed. Actors carrying on lanterns, torches or other such specific properties did so to effectively illustrate location and its specified lighting state. There was little space for any scenery as we know it. The language of the playwright embellished place and time.

Costume design and its class detailing was highly appreciated and an expected spectacle. Properties with detailed significance heightened the imaginative settings. An increased intimacy between actor and audience comes about by the galleries being of a reduced depth. The theatrical style termed as 'romantic' is associated with the Elizabethan thrust and the 'inn' yard.

There are now many theatres that are derived from the original thrust stage. They offer modern facilities with advanced technological capabilities. These thrust stages may offer a fly tower for scenery and lighting. They may be flexibly interchangeable to a proscenium style format. These facilities offer audience intimacy, along with some technical wizardry.

The modern thrust enables design to become more involved visually. The thrust stage makes sculptural demands on design. Through sculptural intervention, design links the areas up-stage and down-stage. With an audience viewing one another through or across the acting area, there develops an unusual relationship and unique bond. This is seen with greater effect within the theatre-in-the-round.

The Proscenium Stage

The proscenium divides the audience and acting space into two separate distinctive parts. This architectural format has direct links to realistic settings. It helps to create actual physical illusions of reality. It enabled theatre to take on great illusory feats.

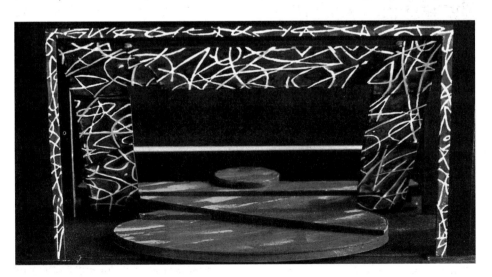

Finished model showing a proscenium stage with 'false proscenium'. Search for Signs of Intelligent Life in the Universe. *Alberta Theatre Project.*

Finished model on a proscenium stage with 'apron' extension. The cut-away walls could be reconfigured or removed for other scenes. Blood Wedding. *Arts Educational Drama School.*

The audience is encouraged to suspend their disbelief. The format with technical facility supports such full-hearted illusion making.

The dividing wall between audience and the acting area consists of a proscenium arch – an opening framing the view of the stage. This may be curtained off by a fabric fire-proof curtain, or house tab. This curtain conceals the stage, masking scene changes.

Constructed within the dividing wall may be the 'iron' – a fire-retardant solid curtain. The 'iron' produces a seal between the two areas. By law, it is lowered and raised once during a performance, either pre-show or at the first interval.

The proscenium may have a stage extension or 'apron' that projects out toward the audience. The apron is at stage level. The value of the apron stage is to bring the play's drama further down-stage through the proscenium, making more intimate the experience for the audience.

Up-stage of the proscenium arch are the technical facilities for scenery, lighting and mechanics. These may be highly sophisticated. With such

The finished model 'truck unit' for Act I of The Importance of Being Earnest. *Stratford Festival, Canada.*

(Right) *Tower truck unit with steel deck platform attached showing swivel wheels.*

capabilities there comes opportunity for complex design.

Wing space, found to the left and right of the acting area, may offer areas for storage. Off-stage areas require appropriate masking, made generally of black fabric; they are referred to as 'legs'. The legs run in sequence at intervals downstage through to up-stage.

Scenery may be built on truck units, or set into tracks within the floor, or alternatively rigged to a fly bar and flown.

The audience's sightlines, being front on, may restrict the production to a picture-image format. The limitations created through its distancing effects and artificial formality may not support the writer's intention to speak directly to the audience through the 'fourth wall'.

On-stage are trapdoors, with escapes to beneath the stage. The fly tower above the acting area, with its pulley and cable-suspended fly bars, is manually controlled. They lift scenery through a counterweight system. The lines are operated from a gallery above and to the side of the acting area.

The Studio Theatre

The studio theatre is a box, often called the black-box. Many main theatres have a studio theatre. Studios vary in size, with some offering substantial space for dance. The studio can support productions of differing styles since they are of a flexible nature and impose no personal decorative characteristics. Studios generally have capacity for different seating configurations. They are of a basic nature technically. The ceiling grid for lanterns is often basic scaffolding bars, suspended beneath the actual ceiling. The space above the grid could allow small scenic elements or

The Linden Tree *finished model in a small 'pub-studio theatre'. Arts Educational Drama School Tabard Theatre.*

properties to be flown through a pulley and cable. Scene or set change may be restricted to intervals, with the audience being ushered out. Transitions between scenes requiring change need to be incorporated into the show's style or to be carried out in a state of blackout. Studio doorways affect the scale of the scenery and need to be carefully measured before designing. How actors move about unseen within the space is determined by the designed passage-ways, known as a cross-over. Access to the dressing-rooms throughout the performance may be restricted. Extraordinary ingenuity and inventiveness in design can be seen in the studio theatre.

The Traverse Stage

With the traverse, the audience is divided into two opposing groups that face one another. The performance space passes through the centre. The end walls may provide little space for designed scenery. This format is most like theatre-in-the-round. The floor is of significant focus for the designer. The audience is very much part of the performance and design needs to respect and complement this unifying nature. Sightlines across the stage are of considerable concern. Design is very much an installation of design elements. Costumes and props feature as on the thrust stage. Technically theatres may well be equipped with excellent lighting and sound capabilities.

The stage may be platforms, and exits to off-stage may be through or around the audience sections. With height to the grid, great feats of design may involve a sailor's crow's nest with rope ladders from the deck area, along with drop banners or flags and suspended sail cloths.

Theatre-in-the-Round

The format for theatre-in-the-round places the actor in the centre of a surrounding audience. The entrance for the actor passes through the seating sections. The exit may take the actor to beneath, around and under the stage, to other entrances. The design emphasis is towards the stage floor, costumes, properties and lighting. There may be facilities for small items to fly in from a suspended position. The floor may provide traps for entrance and exit. Tracking units built into the floor may provide facility for easy movement of furniture, or small scenic elements on and off-stage through the actor entrances. Design details are well scrutinized by its audience, such is the intimacy of performing in the round. Design solutions lie in not hampering action and in giving actors the ability to turn and face all members of the audience at any one time.

Since the first rows of audience are generally low, no furniture should restrict the view of action going on beyond. Atmosphere is created in the first instance through the actor and the floor, by dramatic lighting and the addition of environmental soundscapes.

Open Air Theatre

The open air theatre has the stage and audience exposed to the natural elements. Some offer possible canopy protection for the acting area or seating area. Seating is generally unique to the site, and may even involve sitting on the ground. Many open air theatres are incorporated in, around, or in front of an architectural building that acts as a backdrop. The building's architecture may impose a style or character. The play's setting may require this architecture to be incorporated into the design. Some sites accept that what is permanent could be used as a support from which to build. An open air theatre with a more natural environmental backdrop encourages exciting atmospheric design. As with the arena stage there may be potential for the use of animals. Such spaces are often generously linked to the local community that may prove surprisingly resourceful.

The Alternative Space

With imagination and clever application of energy and resources, any space – public or private – has theatrical potential. It takes a team with vision to successfully create theatre in disused or derelict buildings, in quarries, on lakes, in piazzas and on rooftops. Designing for the alternative space is like all theatre work, both extremely creative and risk-taking.

Although the professional theatre may offer good technical facility, there are good reasons and exciting opportunities in favour of using space other than the professional stage. All stage types, including the Alternative, demand skilful handling by the designer. Professional theatres require trained and skilled personnel to manage and run a production. The professional stage is technically sophisticated and can pose considerable danger to its users. It is therefore essential to adhere to strict rules or codes of practice.

Having a safety officer and fire inspector involved in any production is essential practice and law-abiding. Without a good understanding of stagecraft and its practice, both on- and offstage, the risks of injury or damage are greater. Stagecraft needs to be learned, practised under supervision and developed as a skill.

Along with the technical understanding that goes with the theatre space, the designer is required to develop an understanding and appreciation for the physical space – that being defined through its volume, its architectural character and natural atmosphere. To walk the space, as would an actor, begins to reveal spatial dynamics, its issues and potential. Experiencing it invites questions and leads to enquiry.

APPROACHING A THEATRE SPACE

Research into the companies and groups that have used the space. Enquire into the type of audience the house draws in. Research the range of technical design achieved and some of its technical or engineering feats. This research may reveal what is most unsuitable for performance. Perhaps by visiting and testing it acoustically you would find it less than suitable for your performance standards or musical nature.

Build up a file of investigative research, including sketches of the space from on-site visits. Draw and photograph when visiting. All technical documentation from on-site is valuable back-up. Such a foundation supports and broadens your thought process. The ultimate aim is to fully incorporate the production within the building's architectural constraints, exploiting its capabilities and facility.

Some building constraints, such as internal walls, may not allow or support mechanical fixings being attached. A building's technical limitations could well impose on the designer the need to exhibit original thinking over problem-solving and construction techniques.

Pop in a Box: *a small-scale touring set without masking. A plywood construction with portable seating and floor cloth.* Director: Penny Bernand. Pop-Up Theatre.

APPROACHING A THEATRE SPACE (*continued*)

When confronted with a venue having no established seating format, designing its layout as part of the set may prove advantageous. With a young audience, the solution may become a memorable part of the show (*see* previous set photo).

Consider the audience and theatrical performance as one. New playwriting often demands that one rethinks the format. Plays might challenge established or familiar theatrical conventions. Play publications often describe how the original production was staged. Notes detailing the stage and set style often accompany the script.

The alternative space or open space has initiated and established new and original presentational styles. These alternative venues have helped establish new writing. Often a remarkable experience in theatre performance is associated with a specific venue. They may be inseparable and inextricably linked.

New play-writing challenging design. One of four plays run in repertoire, changing daily. Tuck Tuck. *Director: Bob White; Lighting: Harry Frehner. Alberta Theatre Projects. Photo: Trudie Lee.*

6

THEATRE SPACE
DEFINED TECHNICALLY

E ach theatre stores a set of techni-cal drawings. From these, copies are made for distribution to the designers. These drawings outline the stage space in measured detail. Each drawing represents a specific view-point. All structural details will be mea-sured to scale. Large theatres may scale down to 1:50, whereas the smaller the-atre will generate drawings at the scale

A 1:50 scale figure with designed steel fencing unit. Materials used are brass, wire and fabric mesh. Design: Alison Chitty.

Phil Owens producing a technical ground plan for the designer using CAD (Computer Aided Design). Guildhall School of Music and Drama.

of 1:25. The smaller venues may have simple outlined measurements. Whenever you receive anything less than finely detailed technical drawings, be sure to visit the space and measure up with your production manager. Do not rely on anything other than good architectural drawings. They should be accurately and clearly defined. They need to depict the acting area, backstage space including the wings and storage space, all height, depth and width dimensions including the understage, and the audience seating with relevant sightlines. Technical drawings are presented in a consistent scale.

The side section may, however, be to a reduced scale from the others. With a fly tower, or with audience seating extending itself some distance from the stage, this drawing will need to be reduced in scale to fit the page size. A technical is usually produced at paper size A1 and a section on A0.

TOOLS FOR TECHNICAL DRAWING

Drawing Board: with or without parallel motion drafting arm.

T-square: Hand held, set alongside the top or side edge of the drawing board. Used to draw in horizontal and long vertical lines. Used in conjunction with a set-square to produce angled lines or perpendiculars. The T-square is placed alongside the right-hand edge if you are left-handed. Keep the base clean and free of tape as it regularly accumulates dust and graphite from traversing across the paper. If your drawing board can be angled, the T-square works best along the top edge.

Set-Squares: Used to create the perpendicular and angled lines. An adjustable set-square is ideal. Solid set-squares offer a choice of: two 45-degree and one 90-degree angle; a 30-degree, 60-

degree and 90-degree angle. Have one of each available if you do not have an adjustable one.

Scale Ruler: These come with a choice of scales on each rule. There is the flat type and the three-sided rule available. Scales most widely used in the theatre are 1:50 and 1:25. Other scales of use are those with ratios that make the object larger in dimension to its own size, such as 1:20, 1:10, 1:5, 1:1.

How scale works is: Example in the scale of 1:25. Scaled to represent at one-twenty-fifth its actual size. For every measured centimetre on a normal rule, the scale converts this into representing 25cm; Example the scale of 1:50. Scaled to represent one-fiftieth its actual size. For every measured centimetre on a normal rule, the scale converts this into representing 50cm.

Protractors: A semi-circular or fully round plastic instrument for measuring off degrees in relation to the 360 degrees in a circle. A half-circle protractor therefore gives 180 degrees.

Curves: Accurate curves are made using either a compass, a plastic French curve, or a flexible curve rubber rule.

Compass: Both large and small compasses are of use. The larger should have an extendible arm to create large radius circles. The compass is an instrument also useful for finding the centre of a line, and for dividing a line into equal sections.

Erasure Shield: A thin metal sheet with various shaped openings, it is placed over the drawing when erasing. It protects areas around from becoming rubbed out.

Erasers: Soft lead markings may be removed with a kneaded putty eraser. It can be shaped with ease. When it becomes dirty, bits are removed and discarded. Firmer lines require the vinyl eraser, or rubber eraser. Small particles of rubber left on the drawing surface should be removed with a drafting bristle brush. Using a cloth or your hand will smear the lead.

Masking Tape: Used to mount drawings on the board. Other tapes are not recommended.

Circle Templates: Useful for drawing very small circles.

Mechanical Pencils: The 'clutch' type pencil is the most useful of drafting tools. It holds the lead through a claw. The metal housing, being of excellent character, holds the lead firmly. Leads are available in a wide range from soft to hard.

Rotary Pencil Sharpener: The companion to the mechanical clutch type pencil.

Metal-Edge Ruler: Ideal for drawing out longer lines, a necessary tool for model-making.

Expandable Tape Measure: The metal sort used by carpenters is ideal, with imperial and metric on the same rule. Enables you to get round equivalent measurements easily and quickly. A most practical tool for realizing dimensions, be it for a doorway, a chair, space between objects, and so on.

Calculator and Notepads.

TRACING PAPER OR FILM

This is a naturally translucent paper that comes in varying gram weights. Gsm 60 and Gsm 90 are suitable for technical drawings. Tracing paper is suitable for pencil work, while the drafting film is geared for ink work. Note that tracing paper is affected by humidity. To a degree it will expand and shrink. When using paper from the roll, it is advisable to cut sheets and lay them flat overnight, before using. Otherwise a drawing left on the board for several days will show some degree of change. This will cause some loss of alignment.

TECHNICAL DRAWING

Scale drawing can represent streets, landscapes, buildings, large objects, set scenery and properties. The technique of scaling down from true size simply enables drawings to be of a manageable size. All scale work is proportionally accurate with the original.

Technical drawings should be kept simple and easy to read. Drawings generally are of two types, those that show the general nature of the object or unit and those that exhibit some detailing.

Lines need to be of a firm hand, of even strength and cleanly drawn. If using a clutch pencil, keep a sharp point with the rotary sharpener. Keeping the same line thickness involves rolling the pencil gently between the fingers as you draw. The line should exhibit even pressure. Avoid resting the hand on the paper or T-square when drawing. Try to use the little finger for contact. Encourage free movement in the shoulder and elbow. Woolly lines are a result of the point becoming too worn, or from an irregular arm movement.

Commence by drawing lines with a 4H lead, refrain from making them dark, these are construction lines. Construction lines are darkened to become finished lines later on. The construction lines need not be erased, faint lines do not always show up through the printing. Always begin with general or formal outline shapes. This encourages accuracy. Place shapes on the page with clear space around, allowing for additional information to be added in later. This avoids confusion by overcrowding.

Work up the overall drawing via construction lines. Start in general terms, then become more specific. Be accurate with your scaled measurements. Work through the drawing progressively, outlining the different views expected. Use construction lines to carry down or across to the next view. One view may refer you back to another, so aim to work views simultaneously. When complete, darken in the finished lines. The outline shapes need to be of a firmer, darker line than those internally. All hidden lines are dotted and of less pressure.

With curves, measure off accurately for radius points. In some cases this may take you off the page. It will still be important to know the radius measurement. When using a compass, sharpen the lead with a bevelled edge using fine sandpaper. Compass lines need to be of the same character strength as the lines they join.

Measurements

Scale drawings require accuracy. Measurements are written in to a 0.000 of the metre since there are 1000 millimetres in the metre and can be written out in either metres or millimetres. Two metres reads as 2m, but measurements of less than one metre will be as 0.000, for example, a half metre reads 0.500, a quarter of a metre reads 0.250.

Aim to be methodical about working over problems on the drawing board. It is the opportunity to get things precise. Technical drawings give you the confidence that measurements will be correct later. When adding in free-hand to technical drawings, aim for a well-executed, formal presentation, with neat and precise presentation.

Circles and Arcs

On any circle drawn, indicate its centre clearly, with fine construction lines for the vertical and horizontal diameter. For the centre make a small cross and draw a small circle round this using the circle template.

Terms Relative to the Circle

Arc: a part of the circumference.
Chord: a straight line drawn through a circle, having a shorter length than the diameter.
Circumference: a curve line equidistant from a point known as the centre that forms a circle.

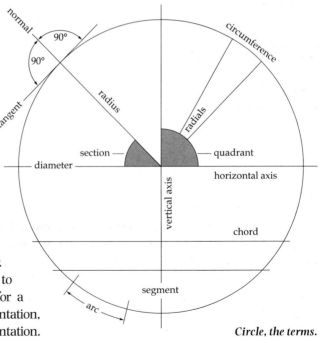

Circle, the terms.

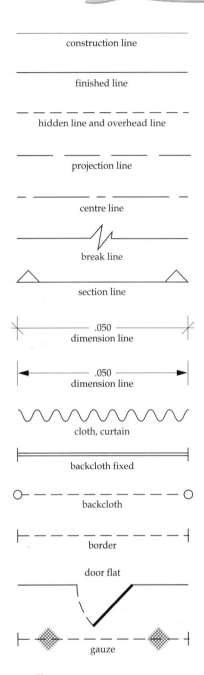

Types of line.

Diameter: a straight line drawn through the centre of the circle and ending with its point on the circumference.

Normal: any line drawn from the centre point that is a radial to the centre of that circle.

Quadrant: a quarter of a circle.

Radius: a straight line drawn from the centre point out to the circumference line.

Radial: a line in the direction of the radius.

Sector: a part of a circle.

Segment: a part of a circle between a cord and its arc.

Semicircle: a half circle in shape, the part of either side of a diameter line.

Tangent: a straight line drawn that touches the circumference and is at a right angle to a normal at that point. Draw first the radius and from that the right angle.

Types of Drawn Line

Construction lines, finished lines, hidden and overhead lines, projection lines, centre lines, break lines, dimension lines, section lines (representing a view taken), cloths, fixed cloths, backcloth, border, gauze, flats, door flats, door, window.

THE LAYOUT

Draw up using an H Lead for the border framing the page. Create a 'legend' along the bottom edge. This will

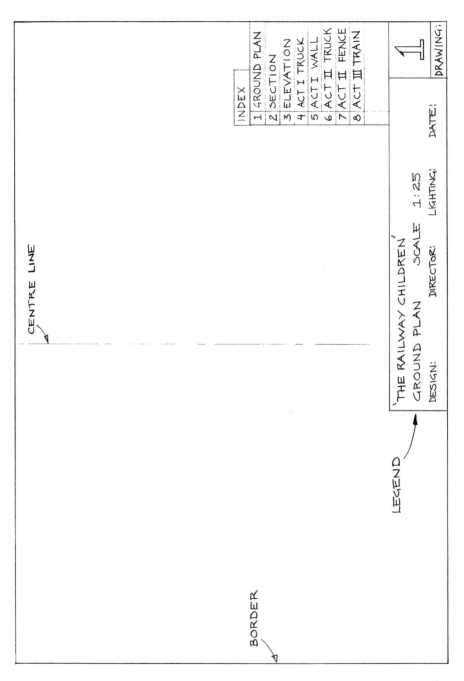

General layout for a technical drawing.

The following text appears within the technical drawing:

CENTRE LINE

BORDER

LEGEND

'THE RAILWAY CHILDREN'
GROUND PLAN   SCALE   1:25
DESIGN:
DIRECTOR: LIGHTING;   DATE;

INDEX
1 GROUND PLAN
2 SECTION
3 ELEVATION
4 ACT I TRUCK
5 ACT I WALL
6 ACT II TRUCK
7 ACT II FENCE
8 ACT III TRAIN

DRAWING:

house all the main written matter except for the 'notes'. This box will need dividing in two. Create in the right-hand corner a box for the drawing number. This becomes a page number reference. The remaining rectangular box will contain the name of the theatre, name of play, date and year of opening, production company, description of drawing, scale, designer, director, lighting designer, date drawn.

On page 1, include a box above the drawing number; this will contain an index for all drawings to come.

LETTERING

There are some demands made of lettering, the first being for clear, neat and uniform printing in capitals. The single most important aspect of lettering is its legibility. Descriptions need to be accurately worded. Keep explanations simple, brief and to the point. A drawing in need of discussion prior to building should say 'to be discussed'. One that needs further thinking through might say 'to be determined'. The aim is to be directional. Builders and makers need steering, any information that presses upon them your intention is of value.

Describe material for construction, and any material application to that construction. At your best describe the mechanics, more towards what

is expected of a unit. Show hinging positions, and all proposed angles of its intended movement. Clarify whenever possible the demands made upon it by actors.

A variation on the Roman alphabet in capitals will do for all drawing. Lettering to be uniform simply requires practice. Draw out parallel construction lines set horizontal to the page. Use a 4H pencil for these construction lines. Add in a centre line dividing it in two. In all drawings these lines are included, although they are too faint to reproduce. For letters use an HB lead. Draw up with good pressure, keeping the wrist free.

Note the fullness of letters and numbers. Aim to achieve a uniform spacing. The centre line assists in locating the letters. Produce formal precise forms. Do not rush along. Practise with lettering taller and smaller. In all drawings the size of print may vary according to which items are labelled as more important than others.

Practise numbers and their uniform nature of measurement in metric. It is good practice in technical drawing to include the construction lines for numbering when detailing dimensions. This keeps to a formal and uniform presentation. Keep construction lines here very faint.

Either upright or angled lettering can be used. Avoid both types in the same drawing. Keep to a 70-degree incline for lettering when angled.

Line Variation

The thickness and weight of line should vary enough to offer an order or sense of importance. With an HB, H, 2H and 4H and differing pressures the technical should be complete. Prioritize lines and allocate a lead; be consistent in any set of drawings.

Ink nibs are offered in a range from thin to broad; the setting down of a thickness for specific lines keeps presentation clear.

ONE DRAWING AND ONE SCALE

Only under special circumstances should you vary the scale in one layout drawing. The theatre technical should determine the scale. Converting to another scale takes valuable time. Only with specific details in a drawing should there be need to enlarge on the same page.

TECHNICAL DRAWINGS IN DETAIL

The Elevation View: This is the view as seen front or face on. It defines the object two-dimensionally. It shows all vertical planes as outlined on the plan and is to the scale of the plan.

Top View: Placed beneath the elevation this drawing represents its view from above. Carry all verticals as drawn on the elevation down to the top view. Define all thicknesses of walls, mouldings, door and window returns, and other proud detailing. Do not erase faint construction lines from one drawing to another.

Side View: Draw this alongside the elevation, to the left or right of it. With complex elevations it may be necessary to draw both views from the left and right side. These drawings measure out height and depth detailing. Carry through faint construction lines from the elevation to the side view.

Side Section View: You may need to slice an object through to better draw up internal proposed construction. This better indicates the relationships of the parts to their surroundings.

Example: Imagine a window within a wall, that is cut vertically through the centre of the window. Turn it sideways and look at its section view. The side section shows how the window sits into the wall and shows depth detail for both quite clearly. Where the window pane is positioned within the window unit itself is also made clear. This drawing is often used to describe the innermost workings. The solid parts which are cut through are then shaded with diagonal lines

Example: A teapot cut through its centre and drawn would show the thickness of the walls, spout and handle in a

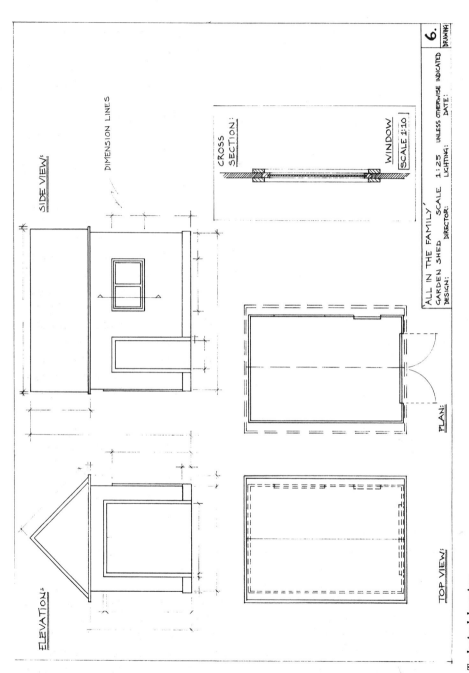

Technical drawing.

cut section view. All the parts cut through would be shaded within since they are solid. The teapot walls would be shaded, but the internal well would not be shaded. The measurement of the internal cavity would be clearly shown as well as how the walls differ in thickness in relation to the handle and spout.

THE PLAN OR GROUND PLAN

The plan view is from above, looking down upon the stage floor or deck. This view will detail all significant architecture above the stage, as well as that which sits on stage level and below. The drawn line and its characteristics reveal what is hidden from that projected. The height of detailing should be indicated in measurement. Architecture above the stage may include the fly gallery, suspended walkways, the fly tower walls, fly bars and protruding walls. That beneath the stage is detailed in fine dotted lines. Trapdoors and 'bridge' platforms are of solid line. Orchestra pit and passage doors under the stage are with dotted line.

The plan shows the permanent walls of the theatre as heavy solid lines, often with a series of parallel angled lines filling it in. This indicates a solid cut section of a wall. The proscenium, side walls and rear wall are included.

Doors are noted with their direction of opening indicated. The scenic dock with its 'lift' will be drawn with a cross diagonal line through its corners, indicating an elevator platform. The width of all exit doors, in relation to scenery 'get-in', are crucial measurements. The front row of the audience should show the two extreme seats both left and right, positioned for sightline reference.

Fly bar positions from up-stage through to down-stage are indicated by the position of the bar ends. The fall of an 'iron' or safety curtain will be represented by two solid lines showing its depth. A tracked house curtain is drawn draped open, with one solid line depicting the closed position. A cyclorama will have solid lines positioning it on the deck.

The plan presents the whole area as an open clear space with empty storage areas. Pay a visit to the theatre to investigate possible additions to its architecture and storage area stockpiling. What may first appear as an open space on plan, in reality may prove restricting. With a show in repertory the storage areas will be loaded with set and props from other shows.

Drawing Up Over the Ground Plan

Overlay a sheet of tracing paper on to the plan and attach both to the drawing-board. Make sure it is square to the T-square or drawing arm. The plan will portray set design as you wish it placed

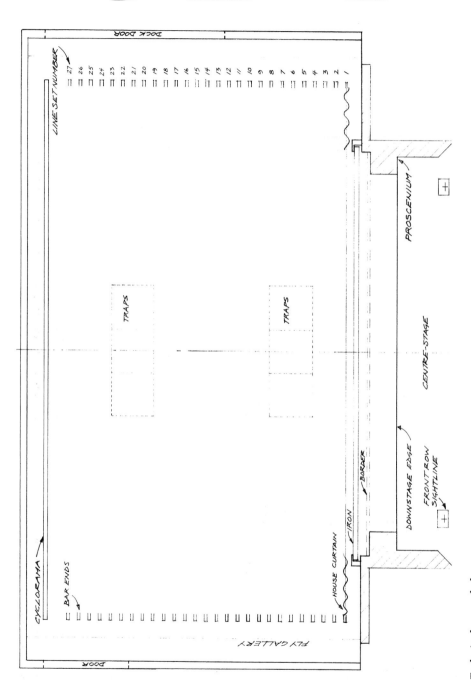

Technical ground plan.

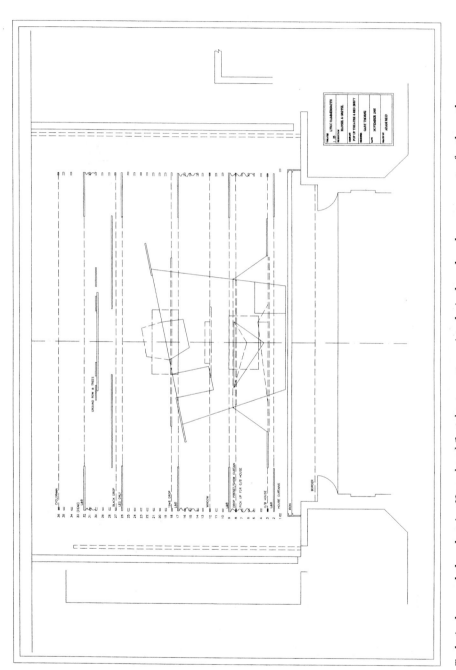

Technical ground plan showing Hansel and Gretel *set, on stage. A technical produced on a computer for the author by Adam Reid.*

on stage. Include all platforms, stairs and detailed architecture such as doors, windows and fireplaces. Measure accurately and always align scenery to the dashed centre line.

Indicate all furniture and property positions. Include standard lamps, footstools, chairs, desks, shelf units, dressers, wastepaper baskets, scatter rugs and so on. Show level variations no matter how slight. With dotted lines draw in lamps, fans and other suspended items as intended. Flown scenery is shown as it aligns with the stage deck. Draw truck unit positions showing their extreme measurements.

A composite ground plan can be drawn. This would show off several scene or act set positions. It is as well to choose a different type line, dotted and dashed for specific scene units so as to relate units and make differentiations between scenes. This makes easier the understanding of overlapping lines.

Any wall unit angled out above the base position should depict the overhead position with a dotted projection line. This enables a lighting designer to anticipate and plot accordingly.

Stage management in preparation for rehearsals will measure off from the plan for set and furniture placement. They will tape onto the floor of the rehearsal room actual size measurements. An accurate plan ensures that both you and the acting company keep to what is intended. The actors' daily encounter with these markings keeps them within the limitation you propose. Actors will find the transition to the stage less difficult with these detailed boundaries accurately defined.

Although the lighting designer will see the model and keep photographs of it for reference, the plan needs to supply all relevant information. Lighting design will plot to the plan and section drawing. Show all wall lamps, sconces, set candle positions, chandeliers and standard lamps on their respective tables and walls.

SECTION VIEW

The section is the side view of the stage, as cut through the centre-stage line. It measures out the dimensions relative to height and depth. The section includes seating in detail from the front row through to the last in the gallery or balcony. Any variant in floor level or rake is clearly drawn. Note some theatres have permanent rake stages, or have a collapsible rake as shown on another theatre section. The under-stage level and orchestra pit, along with trap and hydraulic bridge positions are included.

Note the full stage depth with rear storage area, along with relevant changes in ceiling height. Consider the opening and door restrictions as drawn. The proscenium may have variable height openings. This may be with a flown 'header'. The fly tower

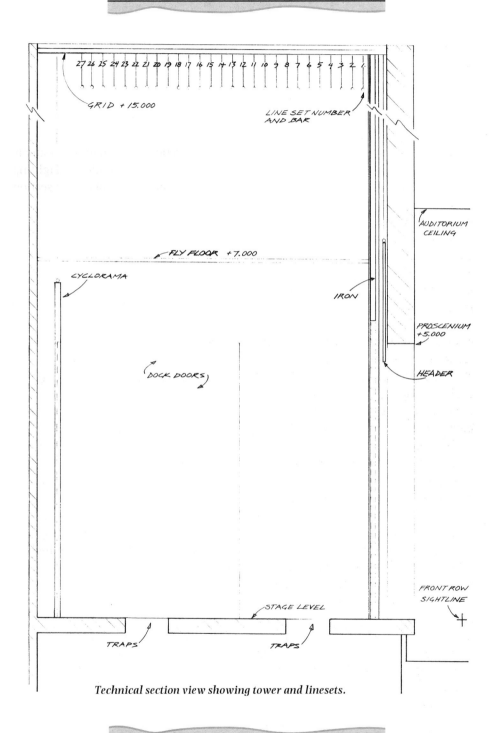

27 26 25 24 23 22 21 20 19 18 17 16 15 14 13 12 11 10 9 8 7 6 5 4 3 2 1

GRID + 15.000

LINE SET NUMBER
AND BAR

AUDITORIUM
CEILING

FLY FLOOR + 7.000

CYCLORAMA

IRON

PROSCENIUM
+ 5.000

DOCK DOORS

HEADER

FRONT ROW
SIGHTLINE

STAGE LEVEL

TRAPS

TRAPS

Technical section view showing tower and linesets.

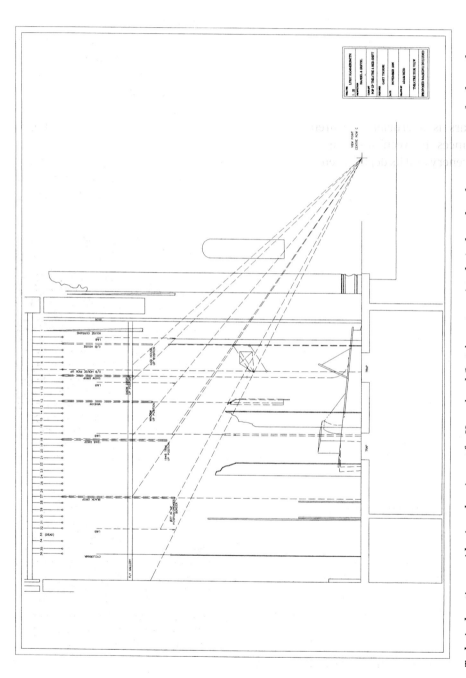

Technical section or side view showing set for Hansel and Gretel *on stage. A technical produced on a computer for the author by Adam Reid.*

perimeters and rigging bars will be shown in their uppermost position. If specific bars are assigned to lighting, they will be defined. The bars number in order starting with '1' from the down-stage position. The spacing between bars is a crucial measurement. Distances between may vary. Designed scenery and its depth when flown need to comply with these restrictions. A flat with 'proud' detailing may put out of action the neighbouring bar. Storage in the fly tower can become a juggling act. Theatres may choose to store stock in the tower, thus restricting some bars from being used. The section enables you to work out the logistics of depth and amount of scenery, to bar allocation. Avoiding LX bars and their lanterns becomes an involved job on the drawing board. Allow sufficient space both up-stage and down-stage for the angle of lanterns.

A theatre without a tower should offer up a suspended grid. Pay close attention to the compromising nature of scenery to lanterns in height.

Drawing up the Section

Place tracing paper over the theatre section and tape squarely onto the drawing board. When measuring do so consistently from a specific point. This may be from the down-stage edge of the stage, or from the back wall. It should be possible to place the tracing paper groundplan between these two.

Remember to turn the plan sideways. Alternatively place the plan at the top of the drawing board, sideways on. Line up the back wall and front stage edge; be sure to have it set square to the section drawing. Carry scenery from the plan onto the section tracing paper.

A section depicting composite scenes needs clarifying. It may be advisable to draw complicated shows with many scenes on separate section views.

SPECIAL NOTE: WHEN DEALING WITH DRAWING UP A RAKED STAGE

Look at a section view with a rake showing objects placed onto its surface. Measure up the plane of the rake from the down-stage edge to locate positions. Take this same measurement from the same down-stage edge and note it onto the deck level beneath the rake. Take a set-square and draw up vertically from this point. Note this important difference: these two points do not align themselves and the steeper the rake the more this measurement is apart from the other.

Set and furniture placement measurements on the raked section do not align themselves to the same measurement on the level stage. Therefore the plan needs drawing up after the section has been clearly figured out. Place all set and furniture on the rake in the section, then align the section drawing with the plan technical and draw up carrying through one to the other.

Drawing up a theatre section using T-square, set-square, scale ruler, eraser and shield.

Flown scenery is drawn as set on the stage with solid lines. The same scenery in storage position in the tower will need to be in dotted lines. The on-stage position to any flown item will show its 'dead' or its lowest flown position. The raised 'trim' position will also be shown. Flown scenery and lighting instruments should not be visible to an audience unless you choose as a concept to reveal the lighting on its bars as a 'look'.

The introduction of soft black 'borders' hide all that which is flown. Finding border positions that act as masking is determined by the sightline for the first row of seats (*see* chapter on Sightlines). Draw a projection line from their eye through to beneath the proscenium opening and beyond. This establishes their uppermost view into the ceiling area. The border's measured height will determine the number '1' position. The front row do not want to see the top of the first border, and its base edge should sit trim with the height of the proscenium. Now draw a second projection line from the eye through to beneath this border and beyond into the ceiling area. Carry on working this way until you have masked off to the up-stage wall.

Sightline projection lines need drawing in above set walls, and through doorways to what is seen above and beyond the unit. You may find that looking up through the door opening, from the front row, reveals too short a masking flat set up-stage. For the audience this will break the illusion.

Take sightlines from the last seat in the balcony. Take projection lines over the top of flats to below and beyond. This may highlight a problem with

This unit stood up-stage of the interior setting. It was viewed through a single door opening. Audience sightlines demanded that the unit be of these dimensions. Dial M for Murder. *Grand Theatre, Canada.*

something being visible on the up-stage side that should not be. Perhaps the top of the staircase up-stage of the door flat is seen, or the actor's head is visible.

On section drawings include a figure, lightly sketched in, as reference. This proves advantageous to first you, then carpenter and technical staff. When drawing up stair units or ladders to beneath a stage, headroom is of crucial consideration.

THE THEATRE ELEVATION

The elevation offers a front-on view, from the audience's point of view. It clearly shows set height and width including that beyond the acting area into the wings. Look for particular measurements made clearer here than on the plan, such as overhanging ceilings and the restricted openings to off-stage. The under-stage may become clearer in this drawing.

Drawing Up the Front View

This drawing is not always necessary. Some aspects of complicated sets may become clear. Simpler sets show straightforward height and width detailing and alignment differences. This drawing is not in any form of perspective. With a raked stage this front view may appear less helpful.

When drawing up the front elevation, the section drawing can be placed beneath to align with this new drawing. Measurement and positions can be carried through from one to the other.

Set technicals: at the scale 1:50 a door's general outline will be represented clearly. However, when detailing the door's hardware or its moulding features, it might prove an advantage to draw up that part larger. By choosing 1:25 or a larger ratio, this will help clarify. However, if the detailing becomes involved, choose another sheet for this, and mention on the first page the new page number.

Finished model door units at a scale 1:25 with substantial detailing. Kiss me Kate. *Design: Brian H. Jackson. Stratford Festival.*

(Below) *Life-size 'template' with measurements indicated and turned balusters.* Three Sisters. *Design: Debra Hanson. Stratford Festival.*

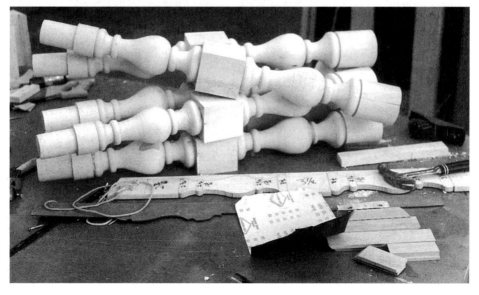

With the smaller detail present this in a framed box or circle. Enlarge according to a new scale and allow enough room for dimension details and a description. Note the new scale within the frame. Take a line with arrowhead to the segment you are enlarging.

Within the legend at the base, you will need to add another scale description alongside the scale for the whole page. Write by it in capitals 'unless otherwise indicated'.

'Actual size' templates are an advantage for mouldings, decorative carved details, stencil work and hardware. Sometimes drawing out onto the wood to be cut is a carpenter request.

SPECIAL NOTE

Drawing in the scale of the theatre technical enables you to draw up, copy, cut and paste onto card to produce the model elevations of set units, all of which are in the scale of the theatre model box. After reproducing a copy simply spray with a fixative suitable for card. Use a fairly generous amount of spray as this ensures that the copy stays fixed to the card when painting up the model.

Actual size model in cardboard for Spilt Milk; *this produced templates for construction.* Design: Gary Thorne and Michael Dalton. Pop-Up Theatre.

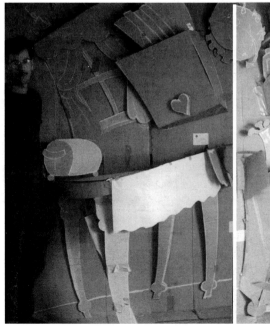

Technical Aims

Do not work out exact construction methods. Supply enough information to accurately define and describe set and properties. Only propose construction preferences. Do not show views from the off-stage side unless seen by the audience. Describe the on-stage intended look. Carpenters apply expertise to methods of building. Keep them informed throughout rehearsal periods of notes that might affect them. Production managers and technical directors assist in solving scenic technical problems. Keep drawings articulate and layout clear. Plan balanced drawings. Workshops will request additional drawings when required. Do not add colour, texture or shading. Only shade-in angled or curved surfaces when necessary to clarify. Avoid repetition when measuring. Step risers and treads need only dimensioning once or twice. Do remember to include the overall dimensions.

COPYING

Reproduction copy centres for architectural drawings require that the original be done on tracing paper or drafting film, the latter being a polyester film. Both are of a transparent or semi-transparent nature. Both should be available up to A0 size, and either in sheets or on the roll. The smoother the surface the less the lead or ink nib will wear down, but the more they will smudge.

The printing process will accept A0 size and will reproduce accurately. There are also photocopy machines available in this size, however the costs of printing are higher than the more conventional dye-line or blue printing process.

With dye-line the printing paper is ultraviolet light sensitive. The tracing paper is placed over the top, fed through and exposed to brilliant UV light. Once exposed, the print is subjected to an ammonia vapour field. This gives the lines their blue-black characteristic. These machines will fold the drawing automatically or they can be hand rolled.

Dye-line printing produces its best results when the drawing is inked in. However, with good pencil pressure, dark lines reproduce well. It is a good idea to do some sample lines and put your local printer to the test. If drawn lines are faint the machine will darken, however the result is an overall shading of darker blue in the background.

Ink drawing pens are expensive. The drafting film is heavy and of a very smooth surface. When an ink drawing is required, first draw up in pencil construction lines. Only use ink when the drawing is completed. Avoid handling the paper; the oil and grease affects the ink's ability to adhere.

I suggest pencil drawings, using variable pencil leads with good pressure and thickness to the lines.

7

SCRIPT ANALYSIS

O pening the first page of a play for the first time is the start of an exciting and adventurous journey. The author has written the work with the intention of it being performed. To read a play is quite removed from hearing it performed. There are aspects of it representing unnatural or unreal time. The play may suspend or stop time. Theatrical time allows for events and situations to unfold dramatically. Time presented may encapsulate years, be presented in altered states both physical and psychological, or look forward and

Various acting areas defined by platform and special location lighting.
A Patchwork Quilt. *Director: Michael Miller; Lighting: Neil Fraser. Polka Theatre.*

(Above) *Jo Richler and Boogie Woogie Bug Band. The puppets and animated set pieces made most of the demands on design. Three actors also needed incorporating into the Scene One set.*

Scene Two offered a quilted layered landscape, hinged country gates, and mechanically animated side wall units. Within was one other pop-up style scene detailed in black, white and silver. Director: Michael Dalton. Pop-Up Theatre.

backward concurrently. Theatre has the resources to imaginatively manipulate, control and alter the perception of time as a means of emphasizing dramatic intent. Whether or not the time and situation presented is actually plausible may not be of issue.

Styles of presentation have grown out of need. The conventions that have been set and their manner of approach have everything to do with content and communication. The development of theatre types are examples of the need for new form to fit new ideas. The constant force behind this is the author's ideas.

Reading a play, musical or opera libretto, for the first time can be hard work. The reading cannot lift it off the page. Not until it is acted out will it become tangible or seemingly concrete. Like music it is written to be performed. Theatre concerns dialogue, expression, gesture and action. There may be very little of each being presented, yet a rich projection of ideas can be communicated. The smallest measure of either has the potential to say a lot. Reading a play involves in part visualizing this. Design involves imagining it 'up on its feet'.

Having to read all the character parts may involve a stretch of the imagination. The content may at first come across as rather puzzling. It is therefore advisable to gear yourself up to enjoy many readings, the advantage being that you can concentrate on different aspects with each read. This approach creates a more thorough investigation,

and puts less pressure on you. It is an advantage to vary your approach by reading aloud or reading along with your director. Allow a generous amount of uninterrupted time. You want to maximize your opportunity to enjoy and explore the play.

Each production of a play will be different. Individuals and groups in society differ, their interpretation and points of emphasis vary widely. Situation, time, place and culture affect us and steer us, as do economic situations along with political opinions and beliefs. There is no one format or best method to perform a play. Results carry along with them an emphasis on content and its issues, along with a stamp of uniqueness for those involved.

Directors may have very good reasons for choosing a play. Historical plays often have special resonance with modern times. Directors and designers may see relationships between the play and another historical period, thus justifying appropriate research to update the play. The play's language however, is not so changeable.

The acting company start first by reading the play aloud while remaining seated. Parts are read by the appropriate actor. It is from this point that the play begins to take on life. The shape it now assumes may surprise even the director. This may have huge consequences on design if the set has already been built, or planned in detail. It is not unheard of that a set and/or costumes, or part thereof, become inappropriate to the play in rehearsal.

The first read-through has its surprise elements. The director and designer should have covered enough ground prior to this moment to avoid there being too big a surprise. It is quite natural that some parts and their characterization might differ from what had been imagined and drawn. For set elements not to work out in the same way may be more financially destructive. Direction and design cannot be planned out totally in advance. Nor would it benefit by it. Throughout the rehearsal process, the designer must remain somewhat flexible in order to consider the changing shape from page to stage. Design needs to keep itself relevant and supportive of the rehearsal.

AN APPROACH TO READING

From the publication note down several of the most obvious and potentially important details.

Edition and Publication: It is essential to know which translation or publication will be used by the director and/or theatre company. These can sometimes differ greatly. Be sure of the publication preferred before buying or borrowing. *Author*: Date of birth and death, country of birth, place of residence if different from origin, list of works credited and their chronological order. The play type: is it a comedy, tragedy, farce, pantomime, and does it fit into a historical type such as those of Restoration, or is it Theatre of the Absurd, Kitchen Sink Drama, or other? Note author 'quotes'. Any insight as to the author's intent or inspiration is of value.

Editor or Publisher notes: These may include translator notes. Introductory notes may be enlightening. This may present the play as having some particular importance historically, or establish a link between the play's subject matter and the author's life. Investigate these through the jacket cover, the introductory notes and foreword. When looking at several publications take notes from each. Establish as clear a perspective on the author and context of the play as is obtainable. Any sense of what you are about to read may make you feel more familiar and at ease.

The Synopsis: This outlines the play's acts, scenes or parts, referring to specifics of location and time. Keep your note-taking to the same format presented by the author.

List of Characters: This list may offer only the names or it may describe them elaborately and in detail. Authors present them as they visualize them. Note the number of characters and whether the author intended actors to double-up on parts being played. Group listings such as servants, pirates or animals may be nonspeaking parts that count as extras.

Check the numbers with your director. Character relationships are of great importance. In Shakespeare's works, the royalty, nobility, court ladies and gentlemen, have titles and significant social positions that shape their character and encourage differences to be made visually between them. Even contemporary plays require the emphasis be put on the internal workings of friendship, family or blood ties, and the hierarchy that goes with position.

Act or Scene Descriptions: This information is found at the start of each section. It may well describe in detail the setting or performance space. Depending on the publication this may be for the set of a production after the author's time. If it is from the author's hand, these notes are of some significance. It may describe the location simply as the author envisioned it. Perhaps this is based on a reality experienced.

These descriptive notes are of course only one way of presenting it. It is a clue to a time and its audience. Have it as a point of reference. Notably different will be the theatre space as depicted by these notes with your own theatre space.

Stage Directions: These are found interspersed throughout the dialogue. They may describe an actor movement in, say, the handling of a property. It may describe a manner being acted out. These notes often say more about the way it was once staged than what is essential. The dialogue will determine for you whether an actor must do what stage notes describe. The director and each actor eventually discover the appropriate action and movement for the character.

Stage directions may appear either in italics or in brackets (He picks up the wine glass, and moves over to the sofa), they may express an emotion (Marion sees red), or may indicate a thought (Albert thinks that John is not telling the truth). Without related dialogue, there is little need to concern yourself with this business. These notes only become relevant when the lines that follow are 'OK, I'll have a drink here with you,' or 'Your shirt makes me want to charge like a bull,' or 'Stop where you are John.'

THE FIRST READ

Read with the intention of experiencing the play as if it were speaking just to you. Narrow down your engagement and make it more personal, more approachable. Aim to read through in one sitting. Take appropriate breaks within the proposed breaks set down by the author. Enjoy the play's language.

Note the first impressions and jot them down in a sketchbook. For now, it is how you sense the play or how you feel about it. This may pertain to the whole work or specific scenes. That which impresses you needs expressing. If something makes you feel uneasy, then describe what kind of uneasiness.

If it feels cold, brittle, or icy try to put an image to it. If sensations occur as reactions to scenes give them a form.

Record alongside the synopsis any seasonal elements. Note the quality of natural or artificial light, its brightness or darkness, the patterns, a time, details to place, along with conditions of life and people within the scene.

First impressions are valuable and need recording. A scene that at first appears absurd and exceedingly funny but in later readings seems less so, may need to rely on your initial impression for emphasis. The audience may need to react in this same manner as yourself. Your recording it, may keep it on course later on.

Expressing a sense of severity or gravity in a scene, might be recorded by mass, volume, light, dark and shade. It may take the initial form of black and white. With more atmospheric impressions colour may better explain how you interpret it. This initial impression may eventually steer your design colour palette. Through recording these initial responses, you build up a collection of ever-shifting and developing interpretations. You need to begin the practice of expressing how you feel and then react in artistic terms immediately. These images are evidence of an interpretation and they speak volumes. Directors look into this process to find acknowledgement for their own feelings and interpretations. Interpret using the foundations of design.

Keep in mind that the play took some time to write. It went through changes most natural to the process of creating new work. Give time to develop your interest for the play. Allow the readings to take you through stages of understanding. Give yourself over to accepting that a good deal of time, plenty of discussion, and much creative work will assist in unravelling its intricate, interwoven nature.

QUESTIONS TO ASK YOURSELF

* Does any one moment have significance over another? In what way does the play build up or down?
* Is there a balance in the emotion throughout? How expressive is this language, how colourful?
* Is there an atmosphere in terms of being hot or cold? How contrasting are the scenes?
* What themes run through each scene? Is there an overall theme?
* Is there an apparently fragile or solid structuring?
* Does the portrayal of life seem to rise, fall, tilt, or sway?
* How can you best describe the various moods created by each situation?
* Are you more focused on one aspect, one issue or one scene?
* What quality of light is there? Are there dark secrets?

* What are the most obvious historical period details?
* Do you feel spatial relations? Are people and scenes huddled together, or spread out and airy?
* Which places from your experience and memory come to mind for one location, then another?
* What does it remind you of?
* How do the issues measure up against one another? Is there weight or mass to them? What is hollow?
* What appears positive, what negative?
* How does the play make you feel in terms of happiness or sadness?
* What may contribute to your favouring an issue or character?
* How do the characters balance out to one another? Do any appear as odd geometric shapes, or remind you of any animal?
* Are some characters more colourful than others, do they have a relationship to texture?
* What friends or family come to mind for characters?
* Is there a quality of line which can best express character and location? What quality of line suggests the differences between characters? Is one more fine and ornate like a scribble, another greyer and woollier like a smudge?
* The tensions that arise between characters can be best expressed in which kind of visual mark?

From this list, many different images should begin to appear. Record a visual answer using art and graphic techniques. Start off on A5-size paper to speed your process along. Work to record quickly what first comes to mind. Then move on to another question. Do not overload one drawing with too much information. Do not labour over a drawing or painting. Sketch it down and move on. Avoid any specific detailing of location or real space at this time. The same with character. If the impression of scale for characters comes to mind, express it in silhouette and through a quick impression. Avoid arms, legs, head and feet details. Title the drawing with what it describes.

FURTHER READING AND RESEARCH

Research the author in more detail. Libraries are your first source. Find out more about the social, political and economic time when it was written. Look into the area where the play is set. Whenever possible use books with photographs or paintings representing the time of the writer, as well as the time and place in which the play was situated.

When a play is remotely autobiographical you will need to do further reading. With historical plays this may involve trips to major libraries, embassies, portrait galleries and photographic archives. Cross-referencing from books on more general subject matter may offer up valuable information. Look into conditions in the whole country; it may reveal something of the writer's life in comparison to others of his generation. Look at what might have influenced the writing and the inspirational subject matter that fuelled it. Newspaper articles of the day may help to clarify your view of the situation.

A Chart for Set and Props

Grid off on paper a chart for each act and its scenes. List first the location as described by the author. This may be simply a living room, kitchen, or garden. Use the dialogue to search out all references to specifics, such as time of day, weather, year, and record all details of actors coming and going. Note what is in the adjoining rooms. List the windows, doors, fireplace, bookshelf and all furniture. Make sure to write alongside, the page, the line and who mentioned it. List chairs or suggestions of places to sit, if they are actually mentioned. Look carefully at the written dialogue for references. If properties are mentioned, observe who spoke about them, or who uses them.

Act and scene charts offer up quick reference to the workings of the play. Plot all essentials relative to action and set demands. On complex plays this avoids having to re-read or remember. The plot becomes an accurate survey of the play.

Examples

Tennessee Williams' Vieux Carré

The setting is clearly described by the author in the introduction. However, it is not made clear until you read the play that the kitchen needs a hole in the floor. Through this NURSIE will pour several pots of boiling water, with the intention that it pours down onto the basement tenants. Without an under-stage level to your theatre, a note about the need for a platform structure in the kitchen will remind you not to forget it.

Time: The period between winter 1938 and spring 1939.

Place: A rooming house, No. 722 Toulouse Street, in the French Quarter of New Orleans.

The Setting of the Play: 'The stage seems bare. Various acting areas may be distinguished by sketchy partitions and door frames. In the barrenness there should be a poetic evocation of all the cheap rooming houses of the world. This one is in the Vieux Carré of New Orleans, where it remains standing, at 722 Toulouse Street, now converted into an art gallery. I will describe the building as it was when I rented an attic room in the late thirties, not as it will be designed, or realised for the stage.

It is a three-story building. There are a pair of alcoves, facing Toulouse Street. The alcove cubicles are separated by plywood, which provides a minimal separation (spatially) between the

Vieux Carré. *A timber framework implying the wall foundations. Platform levels with various steps units. The lower kitchen level with table had a hole in the floor for pouring through the boiling water. The breakdown with paint added to the low life.* Arts Educational Drama School.

writer (myself those many years ago) and an older painter, a terribly wasted man, dying of tuberculosis, but fiercely denying this circumstance to himself.

A curved staircase ascends from the rear of a dark narrow passageway from the street entrance to the kitchen area. From there it ascends to the third floor, or gabled attic with its mansard roof.

A narrow hall separates the gabled cubicles from the studio (with skylight) which is occupied by Jane and Tye.

Obviously the elevations of these acting areas can be only suggested by a few shallow steps: a realistic setting is impossible, and the solution lies mainly in very skilful lighting and minimal furnishings.'

This introduction by the author establishes a preferred approach to production design and its direction. A near bare stage, except for the essential props and furnishings. This is a memory play. It needs to evoke rather than

Preliminary pencil sketch for upstairs bedrooms. Vieux Carré. *Arts Educational Drama School.*

re-create. The flow from scene to scene and the drifting in and out of its characters needs a simple format.

As illustrated, a drama school production varies the vertical height with steel deck platforms. The platform areas signify specific rooms, halls and steps. The preliminary drawings put room alongside room to test out spatial dynamics. The perspective drawings try to visualize it as it might be viewed. The set model develops into floor and wall structuring. The on-stage space is very shallow and the back wall of the theatre wants something down-stage to break it up. The structured period walls are stripped of all facing, revealing the strut-work or the bare bones.

Lighting projections will enhance this skeleton nature. The design seemed to offer enough to suggest the house, without overstating. It appeared sadly neglected and poor from its aged paint-work and grimy look, and sparingly furnished interior detail.

Joe Orton's Entertaining Mr Sloane

The play takes place in the lounge or sitting room of an English house in the 1960s.

Conversation reveals the house was to be part of a row of housing. The scheme never developed leaving this house standing alone. The site over time has become through neglect an ever increasing dumping ground for other people's rubbish. The view out the window is of a picturesque dump.

The interior reflects a low life, it is neat and tidy yet of unusual taste like its inhabitants. There is reference for an alcove to be curtained or shuttered off, a dresser or sideboard, a window with winter curtains, a vase from Bombay, a settee, a fireplace, with interior doors leading to the hall and one to the kitchen.

The housing development is not the only thing to go wrong. Developments between the characters over the three acts reveals much more to amuse and entertain.

KATH makes entrance into the *curtained alcove* in Act One to quick change into a *negligée*. The audience has no idea what she might be doing. She is expected to stick her head out during this change to inspect the record player and the audience should not be any the wiser. Her unexpected appearance fully changed, seconds later, is a great surprise. The alcove by its very nature is a cramped space. It needed to offer access for the 'dresser' to assist. It had also to be designed in such a way as to support the change without us seeing the dresser approach from the offstage side. It had to be light enough and comfortable enough for her to change with assistance. KATH

The rubbish dump in model form. Sightlines determined that the lower sections were not seen by the audience. The armchair gives a sense of scale.
Entertaining Mr Sloane. *Stratford Festival.*

The finished model with cut-away walls and detailed set furnishings. The set broke through the house proscenium and sat over the orchestra pit, making for a more intimate performance. Entertaining Mr Sloane.

The set on-stage showing the close parallel between finished model and the real thing. Entertaining Mr Sloane. *Director: David Williams; Lighting: John Munro. Courtesy of Stratford Festival Archives, 1992. Photo: Terry Hanzo.*

needed to re-enter the room looking neither flustered, dishevelled, nor in a different mood from the one she went in with. The quick-change was timed to the fastest second.

The author creates the setting and emphasizes action and movement within it through dialogue. The evocation of scenic design comes through the character type and their suggested likes.

As illustrated, the design chose to play visually with dynamics between the interior and exterior of the house. Having decided to include the dumping ground outside, design gave way for the house walls to become somewhat eaten away or piece-meal. This allowed the two settings to merge. This dark comedy has an unconventional language, of its time, in the 1960s. *Entertaining Mr Sloane* has elements of farce, therefore a somewhat real setting supported the play's unique characteristics.

Alan Ayckbourn's Absurd Person Singular

The play is very particular to detail and stage direction. It presents us with three couples, each being of a different character type, each couple being resident in three very individual English locations.

Artist rendering for Absurd Person Singular. Act II: The Jacksons.

Synopsis
Early 1970s
ACT I is a suburban kitchen, last Christmas.
ACT II is an apartment kitchen, above ground floor, this Christmas.
ACT III is a Manor house kitchen, next Christmas.
ACT II as outlined through its introduction, dialogue and stage notes portrays it thus:
Fourth-floor flat, door to sitting room which contains a barking dog, door to cupboard, untidy, lived in, trendy, old gas stove, table, chairs, fridge, sink, screwed up balls of writing paper on the floor, open scotch bottle, window with ledge outside, ceiling lamp and much much more.

This realism is uniquely characteristic of the individual couple, and their taste. Act Two portrays the Jacksons, in some decline. The play offers opportunity to reveal class differences, and in so doing one can be set off against the other. Any quality of good and bad design, order and disorder, taste and personal eccentricity, seemed welcome.

The illustration (*see* p.89) depicts an artist's impression of the scene, placing within it all details of potential dressing. The visual information was collectively assembled through research into the period. The preliminary sketches reveal an exploration of the spatial relations as well as period detail. It may not all be used in the model nor on-stage yet it is a valuable reference.

Bill Owen and Tony Russell's
The Matchgirls
A Musical
Synopsis
1888
ACT I
Scene 1 The Corner Cutting Room
Scene 2 Hope Court
Scene 3 By the River Lea
Scene 4 Hope Court
Scene 5 Under a street lamp
Scene 6 Office of the Freethought Bookshop
Scene 7 On the way to the Houses of Parliament

ACT II
Scene 1 Hope Court
Scene 2 Drawing-room, St John's Wood
Scene 3 A meeting
Scene 4 Down by the docks
Scene 5 Hope Court
Scene 6 The 'Waiting Song'
Scene 7 Down by the Docks
Scene 8 Finale

The author's notes request staging it simply by suggestion, relying whenever possible on lighting and sound, along with minimal furniture and properties. He suggests that the opening scene in the factory be a mimed scene. Rostrum levels are considered welcome. Just a browse through the synopsis indicates that it needs to be staged with an economy of design.

Moments throughout the play welcome group being set against group.

The Matchgirls *platform levels with step units and open doorways. The buttresses leaned against the proscenium. Coarse texture and brushwork supported the hard life.* Arts Educational Drama School.

The idea of platforms to make such a divide proved an advantage. Actors were required to shift in and out of scenes quickly and efficiently. The space had to be large enough to comfortably house the chorus of singers. Putting a central opening through the upper level offered a dynamic entrance. The rough brick texture and heavy paint treatment assisted the lighting in creating dynamic mood and atmosphere.

The theatre here has a 'cross-over' immediately up-stage of the back wall, with access doors at extreme left and right up-stage. This kept the full depth of this very shallow stage clear of an on-stage cross-over. The back wall was painted to unify with the design.

Steel deck platform units with scaffold legs cut to fit assisted in keeping the cost down. The facing was the only major expense, along with the on-stage steps. House borders and legs in black velour masked the off-stage surround in the wings and ceiling. Exit steps off the platforms to the wings proved the only real problem, since wing space was tight.

George Furth and Stephen Sondheim's Company

A musical comedy; music and lyrics by Stephen Sondheim

ACT I New York 1970
Scene 1 Robert's apartment
Scene 2 Sarah and Harry's living
            room on the ground floor of a
            garden apartment
Scene 3 Peter and Susan's terrace
Scene 4 Jenny and David's den
Scene 5 Outside in New York City
Scene 6 Amy's kitchen

ACT II New York
Scene 1 Robert's apartment
Scene 2 same as Scene One
Scene 3 Peter and Susan's terrace
Scene 4 A private club
Scene 5 Robert's apartment

Both language and music demanded a smooth flow from scene to scene, at times requiring a seamless link to the next scene. The comings and goings of characters, often in full company, throughout a scene's intimate focus seemed to need carefully orchestrated transitions throughout. Scene change timings were tight. This dictated a stylistic approach. A scene 'set-up' in any realistic manner seemed unfeasible. Any focus on sets would halt the imaginative flow.

A Music Theatre School production introduced flown gauze screens, variably suspended across the stage width and throughout its depth. Panels flew to form variety in formal configurations. The focus was altered within the acting area from scene to scene, the flying movement was done with lighting to complement the musical flow. The gauze screens appeared either translucent or solid, giving opportunity for actors to assemble behind them, prior to their scene, without being the key focus, until they were lit from behind. The stage floor was of levels, blocks and platforms. Within two of these platforms were units like drawers that slid out to offer a bed and a pair of benches.

CHARACTER CHART

Regardless of whether or not you are designing the costumes, it is a good idea to create this chart. It reveals what is mentioned, through the dialogue, of character. This will directly affect your judgements concerning set design associated to character. Character and location are inextricably linked. This chart depicts what characters say of one another, and think of themselves. It also relates action to article.

List the characters' names down the left-hand edge of the page. Do the same across the top edge with the same names. Between the names draw lines to divide them, horizontally and vertically. Names connect across to one another. The same name on the side and along the top meet, offering a boxed space to record what that character says and implies about himself. Include the page and line number, the act and scene number with each quote. When characters reveal something about other characters record this in the same way. Details like: 'I have no one to live for anymore, only you'; 'you look worn out, a victim already'; 'she's so very strict concerning that sort of thing'; 'he's such a misery'; 'you shouldn't say that sort of thing to a married woman'; 'you're a plague, a foul dog gone mad'; 'I'm freezing!'. Some expressions may be much more direct and straightforward like: 'your blue shirt'; 'the red curtains'; 'your clean and tidy room' and so on.

These fragments pieced together help establish character. They initiate the search into developing an image. People's relationships, their familiarity with or misunderstandings about one another shape the play. These dynamics are the way in. They offer foundation and structure. It must be believed that an author puts every word on the page for a purpose, an aim. Design supports relationships of all kinds.

NOTE

Costume quick-changes require that you design the set to best accommodate this with the greatest of ease. There is opportunity in placing dressing booths on stage near exits or entrances. However, there needs to be a logical thinking-through so that actors arrive at their second entrance without showing tell-tale signs of having done a marathon run round the outside of the theatre. The on-stage 'technical dress rehearsal' will establish timings. Yet the director will expect design to have appreciated this in real measured terms.

Further Examples

John Guare's The House of Blue Leaves

The play takes place in an apartment, in Queens, New York. It is 1965 and it is cold.

The two Acts involve eleven characters, three of which are a family: a father, mother and son. The essentials are the window and its cage, the couch, the suggestion of the main door, doors or passageways to other rooms off-stage, and the piano. However, the positioning is open to interpretation, determined by the constraints of your theatre. John Guare mentions they have lived here for eighteen years, yet it still appears they have never totally

The House of Blue Leaves. *The cluttered, unsettled look complemented the lodgers and their peculiar ways.* Arts Educational Drama School.

unpacked. It is a messy place, with loads of specific clutter. The odd nature is relative to the occupants and events that unfold.

The Drama School production suggested the doors, placing them through corridors out of sight-line. An unpacked look was achieved through stacked boxes, which were cheap and effectively masked the corner joints of stock flats.

Henrik Ibsen's A Doll's House

1879. The action takes place in HELMER'S house. Three Acts.

ACT I

Scene: 'A comfortable room, furnished inexpensively, but with taste. In the back wall there are two doors; that to the right leads out to a hall, the other, to the left, leads to HELMER's study. Between them stands a piano.

In the middle of the left-hand wall is a door, with a window on its nearer side. Near the window is a round table with armchairs and a small sofa. In the wall on the right-hand side, rather to the back, is a door, and farther forward on this wall there is a tiled stove with a couple of easy chairs and a rocking-chair in front of it. Between the door and the stove stands a little table.

There are etchings on the walls, and there is a cabinet with China ornaments and other bric-a-brac, and a small book-case with handsomely bound books. There is a carpet on the floor, and the stove is lit. It is a winter's day.

(A bell rings in the hall outside, and a moment later the door is heard to open. NORA comes into the room, humming happily. She is in outdoor clothes, and is carrying an armful of parcels which she puts down on the table to the right. Through the hall door, which she has left open, can be seen a PORTER; he is holding a Christmas tree and a hamper, and he gives them to the MAID who has opened the front door.)'

The play takes place over three days, the last being Christmas day. The country is Norway. The HELMER family home is of middle-class character. The husband TORVALD works in a bank, has received a promotion to Manager, a post he is to take up at the beginning of the new year. NORA is the housewife; there is a NURSE for the three young children and a HOUSEMAID.

What appears as a happy marriage is one troubled with secrets. The struggle centres around NORA. Women of this era were expected without question to conform to society's constraints, especially within a marriage, making them powerless. NORA is driven, some suggest by naivety and a liberal wilfulness.

Research reveals lighting is through oil or gas lamps and candles. Without the medical advances of penicillin, sickness and death were close at hand; vaccination was distrusted by doctors, and it is said it took a cast-iron constitution for a child to reach school age. It was a fifty-four-hour working week; paying off and keeping a home was every man's ideal. Mortgaging or selling was a tragedy. Home was security, success, and a place to be crammed with the precious clutter of one's life. The toilet was in the form of the chamber pot, and the bath tub was pulled out in front of the cooker once a week.

A typical day for NORA begins before the rest of the family arise, with having to supervise the MAID seeing to the fires being cleaned and re-started for the baking of bread. At 6:45 the husband and children dress and splash cold water on their faces from bedroom basins. The children's clothing is made by their mother. Breakfast, once prepared, frees the MAID to go on to the day's washing; in two hours it is on the line. NORA takes charge of cleaning the oil lamps, with their fragile glass chimneys. The MAID prepares a huge

NOTE

1. Begin to imagine that a door mentioned may be successfully placed in an off-stage, out-of-sight position. This may be through a hallway or suggested passage or simply be off behind side masking. Door sounds either live or recorded can assist in giving the impression of it existing.

2. The same may be applied to a window unit. Noting down the mention of a window does not force you into having to supply one. There are other ways around this through effective design. The actor may mention going to the window and remarking on the weather. A fabric lace or gauze hung decoratively on-stage, might suggest it along with effective lighting through projection. A projected window through a Gobo could indicate shape and panes. Equally successful may be placing the window imaginatively between the acting space and the audience. This gives the actors a direct contact with their audience.

hot meal for midday; NORA dusts the parlour and after enjoys the making of bread dough which will sit to rise overnight. The maid irons with flat-irons heated through by sitting on the cooker, while NORA may do mending, needlework, embroidery, beading, crocheting, tatting, dress and handkerchief trimming, doilies, mats or antimacassars.

Richard O'Brien's The Rocky Horror Show

End of *Scene 1*:

NARRATOR. 'I would like (he pauses and finds a huge dusty tome which he takes) – if I may – to take you on a strange journey. (He reads) It seemed a fairly ordinary night when Brad Majors, and his fiancée Janet Weiss ... (two ordinary healthy kids) ... left Denton that late November evening to visit a Dr Evrett Scott, ex science tutor and now friend to both of them ... It's true there were storm clouds, heavy – black and pendulous – toward which they were driving, it's true also that the spare tyre they were carrying was badly in need of some air – but they being normal kids and on a night out – well – they were not going to let a storm spoil the events of their evening. On a night out ... It was a night out they were to remember for a very – long – time.'

This introduction leading into the following scene has some relationship to 'Once upon a time'. It is beautifully simple and imaginatively presented. It stirs the imagination and memory through the simplest of means. It has the effect of stories round a campfire. Stormy clouds passing over the moon along with nocturnal sounds evokes the full setting. Here the narrator vividly depicts the situation and its developing atmosphere. The scene is set for the entrance of Brad and Janet.

There is no need for a complicated setting. With the narrator being a constant character in the play, he may require some set position, perhaps to the side of the acting area. Reading the whole play and adapting it to your space would determine his relationship to the acting area.

DETAILED RESEARCH

Historical research is invaluable. Any period referencing adds to the understanding of the play. It may prove of value to observe previous production photographs and/or illustrations. The life and times of an author together with the play's period and setting must entail some link.

Note that prior to the invention of photography you have to rely on illustration, engravings, paintings and drawings, along with written documentary evidence socially and politically.

Different-aged characters may display aspects of their own time. Parents and grandparents show some signs of attachment to a time unique to them. This may take the form of accessories, dress detail or set detail. They might appear somewhat 'old fashioned'. These different characteristics should at least be considered as part of the design process.

No home or workplace, whether public or private, is a state-of-the-art representation of its time. The home and a room's furnishings often display a variety of period detail. How you embellish and style this depends very much on the focus of ideas within the play. A farce might open the door to very stylistic touches, centred round the decorative arts. Updating a play requires careful cross-referencing to find parallels to social, economic or political issues, to objects and accessories for both set and costume.

Visiting an author's place of work may reveal a library of information. A play's location might be well worth the trip to see. Local setting, the architecture, the colours within the landscape, the sense of community may draw you into seeing or feeling something special.

Research through embassies for foreign authors. Major cities have foreign country libraries. Look at all cultural expression for the author's and play's time. The musicians and writers of the period offer insight. The same with cinema and movies, documentaries, radio interviews and culture programmes. Folklore and ethnic costume and cultural artefacts have deep associative relationships to some period plays, dance and opera.

Seek out a wealth of research, study it with your director and file it appropriately in scrapbooks and sketchbooks. This library of visual information becomes your stepping stone to design.

8

THE THEATRE MODEL BOX

This three-dimensional model directly relates to the technical drawings supplied by the theatre. The scale is the same for both. The model box represents the overall space, defined by its architecture. This construction relates the performing space to the wing space, back-stage, the fly tower, and the audience seating. It is a realization through a precise scaling down from the original architecture. The space with constraints and limitations is clearly visualized. Such a scale model is physically manageable making it easy to relate to. The model box is a vehicle for entering the space. It is the foundation and framework into which all design ideas are put. It becomes the stepping stone to the sketch model through to the finished presentation model. Design needs to 'fit-in' to the model box. This concerns the physical proportioning of all set elements to the whole space. The model box therefore requires being built with a degree of excellence.

The model box is made from black mountboard and/or black foamboard.

The construction aims should incorporate all affecting architectural detail. Constraints of architecture will impose upon and challenge design aims. Included would be an apron or stage extension beyond the proscenium opening as well as the under-stage level. Side walls and the back wall should feature any protruding elements and dock door openings. If the proscenium has flexibility for the opening arch, it is advisable to build it with the larger opening. This enables an insert to be built and applied to reduce its size – an easier approach when there is indecision concerning which size opening to use.

The model box can be constructed to collapse. Having it easily pack away makes it all the more portable. It is often on the move from place to place. Once constructed it is always the centre of attention when in meetings with the director. All ideas are sounded out in the model box. There is a great risk when this approach is overlooked or ignored. If design fits in and looks right within the model box then it will most surely fit in on-stage. The accuracy of measurement between the model box and the presentation model within it is of great concern. Once a set is built and put on-stage, the comment should be 'Well, it looks just like the model, only larger.' The technical drawings which develop from the model ensure that the set then most accurately measures up to the theatre. If the set and furnishings 'look' appropriate in scale and balance in themselves and to the model box, then the work is being steered in the correct manner to its end.

The model box becomes a playground, an experimental laboratory. The significant view into this space is always from that of the audience's point of view and sightline. Any idea can find some representational form within it, however they need to make themselves relative in the first instance to the play and secondly in being visible to the viewer. The model box supports an aesthetic, it therefore wants to be in itself a fine piece of work. Since the theatre is considered a black box, there is no application of colour to the model box. If a theatre has a gilt proscenium surround it is not a requirement to include this. The focus is generally on the acting area, the set and its furnishings. When the house lights fade and the stage lights come up, the eye becomes focused away from theatre detail.

CONSTRUCTION OF THE THEATRE MODEL BOX

Cutting

To cut through card and foamboard requires the use of an X-acto blade, surgeon's scalpel, or matt-knife. The finer the detail, the thinner the blade to be used. For heavy card a Stanley knife is recommended.

CAUTION

All cutting blades are *extremely dangerous*. Always use a steel rule to cut against. If it does not have a thin cork backing to keep it from slipping, run a strip of masking tape along its backside. Always keep fingers well clear of the metal edge. Lean over your work, to see exactly what you are doing. When holding the rule, let the palm of the hand rest firmly on the card. This will secure the rule from moving as you cut along its edge. Cut slowly, with light pressure to score the card. Cut through again with firmer pressure. Allow for many cuts to penetrate. Do not try to to cut through card in one attempt. This may put too much pressure on the blade causing it to snap. Work on a clean uncluttered cutting board or prepared surface. You will be less likely to injure yourself if there is order to your table top, along with good directional light from above.

Start with the stage floor. Work directly from the theatre ground plan. Consider including the acting area, wing space to the left, to the right, and the up-stage area. Include the apron or stage extension. If there are alternate configurations to the down-stage lip, build them as separate attachable units.

Place the technical ground plan over your card or board and pinprick through all corners indicating the wall positions, doorway openings, dock doors, centre line at a down-stage point as well as up-stage point and proscenium opening. It is advisable to note the thickness of walls. Indicate the trap positions and other floor details where necessary. This approach makes easy the transfer of information from the plan drawing to the card. It saves time measuring and is very accurate. Consider the extreme boundaries to walls before cutting. Remember that foam-board thickness representing the walls needs to be included. Cut out the defined perimeters. Construct the floor into a platform by giving it height, regardless of the theatre having an under-stage. This offers a firmer foundation or base, one that will not warp. Construct the under-stage walls from the same board. It need not be higher than 0.05mm.

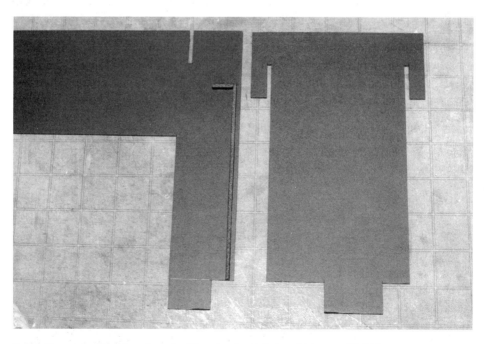

Left is the proscenium foamboard with cut-out notches and tongues. Right is the side wall with the same. Model box construction by David Neat.

Glue them to the outer underneath side. Reinforce with cross walls as this helps to resist internal warping.

The proscenium wall should be constructed next. Take the front elevation and pinprick through the essential details. The outside dimensions should be the same as the floor width you have just made. It is not necessary to include the full height of a fly tower in the model. Build the height to include the theatre border's full height. This would be with a trim on the base of the border aligned with the proscenium opening. This enables the model box to feature borders that would clearly represent the masking intentions you would wish for.

A proscenium stage with balcony box seats positioned on or into the auditorium walls that hug the proscenium, should be included in the construction. These balcony boxes may become part of the show. This is a matter to clear

NOTE

Include tongue extensions to the base and sides. The tongues protrude down from the base edge. They should be positioned either side of the proscenium opening. These tongues will slot into the floor unit. Notch openings are cut into the floor to accommodate these.

The side wall pieces require the same tongue extensions included on their bases. These too fit through a notch opening on the floor. The side walls also need tongue extensions included on their side edges. These tongues are positioned at the top of the edge, on both sides of each wall. These two tongues will eventually slide through notches that will be cut within the proscenium wall and in the back wall.

The black foamboard front, side and back wall for the model box.
Construction by David Neat.

with the production manager and front of house.

Take the section drawing of the theatre. If it is at a different scale from the others, you will be required to do some measuring up to mark off on the card. Made to the same scale follow through with the previous procedure. There are two walls to construct here. It is practical to build one then use it as the template for the other.

If your card has white on one side and black on the other, remember to reverse the first wall before using it as a template. This keeps the inside of the model box side walls both black.

Any projected architectural details need to be cut and constructed onto the wall surface prior to the whole being assembled. Cut out all doorways and dock doors leading off the stage.

Fly towers need suggesting, as mentioned previously, only up to the top of the border. With some smaller venues the theatre model box may include them in their full height. This is a good idea when there is a lot of flying to be done. It may assist in representing how tightly fit the flown units are when in storage above the stage.

For either model, take the ground plan showing fly bar end positions and photocopy this twice. This will be cut and pasted to card. Then assemble it onto the top inside or outside edge of the side walls. Viewed from above the model will then have in scale the true positions of the bars thus indicated.

Suspend all flown scenery from a thin wood batten using piano wire to represent vertical cabling. The wood batten will sit across and onto the two shelves with bar markings, thus aligning the batten to the bar number.

The two seats at the extreme left and right in the front row may need to be included. Theatres with a thrust stage, and those in-the-round may want the seating sections included. A model box with flexible seating needs the options proposed, so discussion can centre round the model and possible configurations. Do not close in all sides of the auditorium, remember you need to get eye level down to see the front row view.

Any gluing should be done using PVA or carpenter's wood glue. A thin, neat line of glue applied to one edge or surface will do. The pointed spout of the glue pot enables you to work neatly and accurately.

The back wall can be cut using the proscenium wall as a template, unless there is a big difference between the two dimensions. However, the width should be the same for both seeing that they sit on the same floor plan. Include two tongue extensions to the base. These will require notches to be cut into the floor. The proscenium and back wall require notches to be cut vertically down from their top edges to accommodate the tongues that are part of the side walls. This should produce a stable and conveniently collapsible model.

9

CONSTRAINTS

AN APPROACH TO DESIGN

Before Design and Production

Decisions concerning production begin with the director and designer. The proposals for contract, budget, the venue, scale of production, workshops and actor numbers come hopefully together as a package. More often with small-scale and fringe productions, it is vaguer than this. Ask questions and get answers.

There is always compromise with a production. Flexibility revolves round choice of construction material, the approach to construction, the staff and skilled labour capabilities, facilities and more. The attitude that should prevail is 'It is necessary or essential for the production', not 'This is how things have been done before ...'.

CONSTRAINT, ALLOCATION, AND TAKING CONTROL

Working with a small budget requires innovation and ingenuity. The main concern is for the practical management of money. When introduced to a budget, make investigations into the sum allocated for design. Speak to the production manager or technical director concerning the budget. Enquire into what other moneys have been allocated to the production. Ask if sums are set aside for transport, hire of lighting and sound equipment, seating, or for set, props and costume departments. Ask if labour costs come out of the design budget. Be sure to clarify where your design fee comes from, how much that may be, as well as what the real duties are for that fee.

What initially may look like a healthy sum for design may end up much slimmer when appropriately allocated. The budget breakdown should begin after visiting the theatre. Throughout the process the production manager will continually print out an update of spending. Know where money is going. Prioritize and spend appropriately.

The process of design is long and involved. There is considerable research, drawing, model-making and lengthy discussion with the director prior to production. Decision-making takes good time. It requires clear-headed imaginative thinking. Approach to material and construction requires familiarity and experience.

Concern yourself with all aspects of design and production. The overall picture ultimately offers a more calculated and balanced position. Observe the technical and artistic abilities of individuals. Anticipate results and make judgements on capabilities. Steer decisions whenever possible, as to who might build and paint a unit or article. You might prefer something built by the properties department to be painted by the scenic artists. An elaborate carving may be more cost-efficiently produced by an out-of-house maker. Weigh out the odds of time, money and expertise. Make considered observations. Discuss with the production manager, and decision-make with your director.

Painting on a wood-grain effect is less expensive than building with wood. Creating theatrical effect opposed to using the original material will require 'scenic artists'. Paint on canvas that becomes stretched over the stage floor may prove a financial advantage over hardboard,

Marjorie Daw *Scene 2: in the fish bowl, book-hinged flats opened out to another scene. Director: Penny Bernand. Pop-Up Theatre.*

Blood-red curtains effectively parallel the ghastly deed being plotted. Murder in the Cathedral, *1986. Director: Zoe Hicks; Lighting: Jim Bowman.*

Finished model out of the model box. Platform stage extension, false proscenium and truck set unit. Lettice and Lovage. *Alberta Theatre Projects.*

cut, painted and assembled. Weigh out the odds for different approaches.

Take apart the budget time and time again. Familiarize yourself with the buying and spending process. Decision making and prioritizing go on through to the opening night. Aim to get value for money.

Director and Designer Decisions

Budget breakdown and the allocation of sums will largely be determined by the concept for your production. Your approach to presenting the show and where you might prefer to lay emphasis becomes a negotiable concern between the director and designer. Initial questions concern the overall aim and the play's essentials.

Stylistically one may choose to sacrifice one element of design for another. Through the process of elimination, one begins to form a direction. Consider properly the options: made costumes and properties, no set; built set, hired costumes and borrowed properties; made properties, hired costumes and no set; or other. Propose a realistic breakdown by thinking clearly about ambition and realization.

Research Available Stock

Know your theatre space, its potential with regard to stock flats, soft and hard cloths, furniture and property collections. See what is on offer as free material from previous shows. Look at the costume store. Ask for a printout of basic set and stock materials, such as black legs and borders, drop cloths, gauzes and any hard scenery. Ask about alternative seating and the cost regarding alternative seating configurations.

Consider the scale issue between main stage and size of your production. This may steer you to immediately adopt a false proscenium to reduce the scale and costs.

CHALLENGING THE PLAY

The term 'box-set' is regularly used to define a design in which walls surround the acting area on three sides. It has a conventional nature and aims toward realism. The limitations of such a set are seen in its solid, matter-of-fact nature. It has a tendency to simply state the obvious. The solid wall, with decorative detail, and structured door and window constructions, may not prove to open out a situation.

The traditional box-set presents a literal interpretation of an imagined room. Without a good measure of intrigue and a great measure of accurate fine craftsmanship, it can sit on the stage with oddity. The problems are in the removal of the ceiling, suggesting believable adjoining rooms, and opening out the side walls to

One of four plays in repertoire. Flown flats with projected texture, down-stage of a cyclorama. All Fall Down. *Director: Mary Vingoe; Lighting: Harry Frehner. Alberta Theatre Projects. Photo: Trudie Lee.*

angles which benefit sightlines. The furnishing arrangement becomes complicated. The view outside the window also becomes a painterly impression due to limited space. Small budgets make this task problematic. Set furnishings are expensive and hard to find in period especially when they need to match stylistically.

Some plays make it somewhat difficult to break away from flats and traditional architectural detail. It is possible, however, to develop a box-set into conveying something other than the most literal of interpretations.

Elaborating on or expanding a theme to encompass the whole play may prove more effective. Such an emphasis may open it out to more painterly results. A cloudy sky effect painted onto the interior walls might broaden out the horizons. This approach may satisfactorily merge two ideas. Think of the room as a painter might approach a broad canvas. Architrave details may be combined.

The painterly arts offer up rich resources and reference. Note the artists in the author's time, and those with relative concerns. Merge the outside world with the inside. Or deconstruct the interior to a more fundamental simplicity.

Another emphasis is on structural concerns. Think of structure and form in terms of base materials. The elements used to make up the real world in base form may complement the issues in the play. Steel might complement the colder harder-edged realities. Brass or copper walls will suggest warmer harder-edged realities. Associate and make poetic the material to theme or issue. Use stone, water, fire, glass, chrome, rusted steel, plastic, woven fibre both natural and synthetic, and wood. Become familiar with all building and manufactured materials.

Steering ideas away from the most obvious takes time, ingenuity, innovation, and an enquiring attitude. A less literal interpretation favours the audience's imagination. Look at the poetic, metaphorical, symbolic and expressive powers of material. Test out options on the director. Keep an open and broad mind. Visit exhibitions of all kinds.

Clever presentations do not necessarily prove to be effective. They may produce superficial results. Cleverness should only be associated with context to character location; keep it relative to the text.

Using your imagination involves using your memory. Memory is more immediate to an experience. Personal experience affects you deeply. To research imaginatively involves applying your experience to the issues and interpreting them. Design that is interesting reflects personal interpretation and involvement.

Design needs first to be practical and useful. The play is the vehicle for all your applications. The play's essentials need supporting visually. To challenge a play with applications of design enquiry, demands that you keep one eye closely on what is being said, and one

Small-scale design keeping to a theme with bold touches so as to attract the eye away from the school setting. The Nightingale. *Director: Karl Hibbert. Forest Forge Theatre.*

(Above) *Portal openings, raked platform, city ground row, with minimal furnishings. The portals became a broad canvas.* Six Degrees of Separation. *Director: Bob White; Lighting: Brian Pincott. Alberta Theatre Projects. Photo: Trudie Lee.*

One of four plays running in repertoire. Platform units were shared. Projected sky on a wrap-round cyclorama. Johannesburg. *Director: Ronalda Jones; Lighting: Harry Frehner. Alberta Theatre Projects. Photo: Trudie Lee.*

eye on what you are actually saying. This involves passionate involvement together with a critically objective view.

Design's strength can become dominant and distracting. A little goes a long way and the idiom 'Less is more' is quite appropriate. That which hints and suggests provides rich food for thought. Leave room for your audience to imaginatively fill in. They come to get out of the play something special for themselves. Do not overcrowd or overstate. Often what is not said outright but merely hinted at, reveals more. Open any book on theatre design and ask yourself what it is you like most about a production photograph. It might be what it suggests to you, or what it reminds you of, or what it might be.

Take apart the play to reveal structural foundations. Observe the ingredients that make and suggest the play's basic concrete nature. Is nature's season within the play a subtle force? Is the ice on the lake, as mentioned, the most frightening image and what aspect of it is so threatening? Are internal fears related to outside elements? What other forms can ideas take? What forms better encapsulate the feeling of the play?

Be adventurous enough to build up ideas, destroy them and rebuild them. New forms through such reorganization may better suggest the old imposed orders. Fragments and ruins have strong associative powers. Create intrigue, challenge design to invite and initiate adventure and enquiry.

The remains of a sketch model after an initial director/designer meeting.

10

PRESENTATION OF TWO-DIMENSIONAL IDEAS

EXERCISE

Material Required

A4 white heavy-cartridge paper. Gum or paper paste. Coloured pastels and black compressed charcoal. Coloured tissue paper. No scissors. Soft pencils. A selection of colour supplements or magazines from a newspaper. Use only those that do not have gloss paper, ideally those that have a dull, matt paper surface. The photographs and graphic designs on this newsprint quality paper appear grainy. They offer a less sharp, less hard-edged quality image.

Give each question considerable thought, let your imagination run free. There is no trick here nor is there a right or wrong way to do this. What you create depends on your spirit of adventure.

1. Choose three different family names, unfamiliar to you, through looking at the telephone directory. Perhaps the more foreign they appear the better.

2. Place these names alongside one another horizontally, across the top of an A4 sheet of paper. Divide the page into three vertical sections.

3. Below each write out an answer to the following requests.

   a. Give them each a first name.
   b. Are they male or female?
   c. What age are they?
   d. Give them a country of origin or place of birth.
   e. Classify them with status: single, married, divorced, living common law, widow, separated, or other.
   f. Are they employed? Or a student? What do they do?
   g. Any personal hobbies or interests?

h. What sort of family background?

i. What are they most passionate about?

j. Give them a height and approximate weight.

k. What is their hair colour? Is it natural?

l. Political interests? Social or community interests?

m. What most troubles or worries them?

n. Describe their character traits? Are they excitable, mellow, highly strung, neurotic, or other?

o. How emotional? Are they hard or soft types?

p. Any ambitions for the future?

4. Now choose one day of the week, one month, and a year.

5. Pick a country, then a city, town, or village within that country.

6. What is the season, and the weather that day? Choose a time of day.

7. These three characters are in the same place at the same time. Where are we? Give a location. Are we inside, outside, is it a public or private place?

8. Why are these three together here? What brings them here? Did they come alone or accompanied? Is it all by chance? Any suspicious reasons behind the meeting? Outline what will happen within the next five minutes.

9. Who is more in control of the situation?

10. Prior to this moment what was each doing and where were they?

11. Who might gain more than the others here? Who has more to lose?

12. What most worries them silently in this confrontation?

13. How will location affect their behaviour? Are there social codes or rules associated with the place? Can one have fun here, be at ease, say what one pleases, do as one wants? What things are forbidden? How differently does place affect the three characters?

14. Name an object best associated with each character, something they might covet and hide away.

15. Are they like any particular animal, in manner or shape?

16. What is the overall mood? What sounds and smells are you aware of, what is the quality of air – is it light or dark, shadowy or intensely bright?

By now you have a well-established situation. You have charted some significant aspects for this moment. Location puts them into a context. There are social pressures here and well-established traditions. Perhaps there are unwanted expectations. What social constraints are you aware of?

COLLAGE ONE

Step One

Close your eyes and picture the situation. Enter the location as if you are a fly. View it from different angles. keeping the characters in the picture. If the image appears vague, appreciate the sense of light, texture and shade pattern. Build up an impression. Concentrate on the overall atmosphere. Consider the coolness or the heat. From which direction does the light come? Are the patterns and rhythms part of the location or have they something to do with character too? Take the colour supplement and begin tearing out colour, pattern, texture, light and dark values that seem to best describe how

A collage expressing mood and atmosphere with form, colour, pattern, texture, line and value. Blackheath Community Opera Workshops.

Collage expressing a spatial interest through line, texture, form, colour and value. Blackheath Community Opera Workshops.

you feel about the situation. Glue them down onto the A4 white page. Keep to a form of impressionism. Capture the atmosphere and mood.

Avoid words or representational commercial images. Use no recognizable objects or products. Play with the pure elements of design. Work the whole page; it is finished when no white paper remains. The only white left should be that which you have glued down intentionally.

Step Two

Once dry, work gently into the collage with soft-coloured pastel. This helps stress or emphasize the most important colour and harmonizes or unifies the image. The pastel wants to blend the collage edges together. Use the finger to blend. The collage represents one aspect of the situation. It may only suggest a sense of rhythm, or degree of light and shade, or spatial interplay of colour.

Collage Two

Step One

Think about the extraordinary circumstance that brings these characters together. Imagine the tensions and dynamics that exist between them. They each have their own textural feel, they each have a sense of pattern, and they must have an inner value between light and dark. Consider their range of differences – from powerful to powerless, happy to sad, tender to brutal, positive to negative. Now again imagine the situation this time concentrating on what patterns, rhythms, light and texture that they each give the space. Their shape can be made through simple textural or linear characteristics. Perhaps radiating from their silhouette is a quality of line. With their individual dynamics in mind, what does each add to the atmosphere? On another page, collage together a sense of the individuals, alongside one another. Keep to a simplified silhouette, no heads, necks, legs, arms, hands, only a simple shape. One will appear taller, one more squat, and so on. Where necessary give them boldness. Emphasize the lyrical, order, chaos, fussiness and so on. As you get on, refer back to the first collage and use some of the same atmosphere to blend your character together. Work the whole page as previously.

Collage Three

Step One

Consider a specific viewpoint. Concentrate on finding the one view that best supports the dynamics between the characters. Is it close up, from a wider angle, or more from above or below? Associate the angle of view an advantage for eavesdropping on their conversation. Is one character in more of a dominant position than the others? What objects are close at hand, what type of furniture is in the room, what is immediately behind, what material is on the floor, are there other people in view, who is smoking, drinking, eating, and what state of dress or undress is each in? What about coats, jewellery, gloves, braces, short trousers, big floppy hats, handbags, table cloth, soft chairs? Is there a breeze? Now place a paper on the table in front, place the pencil tip at centre and look straight ahead, not at the page. Draw up what you see without ever lifting the pencil off the page. Carefully roam from one object to another, explore the shape of each and link onto the next object or character. Concentrate on the contours of the objects.

Step Two

Now consider the outside, the space surrounding this location. What aspects of the outside world seem to ground this situation. Think of the area, the borough, the skyline and the quality of street life. Imagine what might be shaping this situation. Which social forces might also be pushing this situation along? Are there larger, more complex issues? What does this situation remind you of? Are there prejudices driving it, is it manipulated by broader social and political problems in society? Or is this a very isolated moment, quite removed from anything experienced before? Start a drawing that crams in together on the page all these external issues. Make a statement about how you feel about this, include the three characters as small peas in the pod, or as refugees afloat on a raft, or happily singing as they float together in the sky. Surround them with what is good or bad, that lifts them up or weighs them down. Show how the outside affects their inside world.

Be graphic and play with two and three dimensions in a distorted way, like a sort of snakes and ladders display. Work into this with colour and collage; be bold and expressive. Create a poetic image, juxtapose, using symbolism and images with associative connotations. Use words or letters and numbers as part of the structuring, not so much as pure decorative elements. These may serve as undercurrents.

As a project this can be developed quite extensively. Do not rush through each step.

1. Research the location, its city or town. The date determines the period. Find all appropriate imagery for such a place in that time. Research furnishing and prop details. Start assembling a scrapbook of information.
2. Research character type and dress styles. Look at all details from head to toe.
3. Find a face for the character.
4. Consider the kind of theatre space to suit the situation. Draw up some seating configurations.
5. Draw out freehand some more views of the situation with the characters moving about the space.
6. Build a simple black model box and collage into this scraps, as you did with the collage. Add in platforms out of lightweight card. Make a scaled figure for the box. Add in elements borrowed from the previous works.
7. Develop the story further along and do the same in the model box.

11

SPATIAL DYNAMICS AND SIGHTLINES

MOVEMENT DYNAMICS

The Acting Areas

The acting area is divided into sections defined specifically for the actor. The terms are based on the actor's position on-stage while looking out to the audience. Stage-left and stage-right are the actor's left and right. Therefore these terms are the opposite for anyone in the auditorium looking at the stage. Up-stage is that area towards the back wall, with down-stage being towards the audience. Up-centre refers to being in close proximity to the centre-line of the stage, so too with down-centre. Other terms are up-right, up-left, down-right and down-

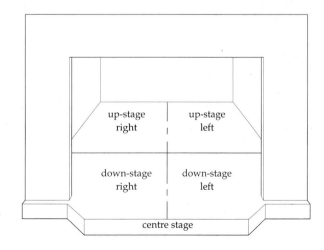

Acting terms in relation to the actor facing an audience.

Raked stage platform and backdrop shown in isolation without its model box and masking. Wizard of Oz. *Polka Theatre.*

left. A director always uses these terms. It is common terminology for everyone.

Dividing-Up the Acting Area

An acting area may be planned so as to accommodate several different locations. Boundaries may be defined simply through focused lighting. Minimal furnishings can suggest place most effectively. Platforms also divide up and make separate the areas. Levels of con-siderable height introduce greater divisions, they naturally suggest a greater distance therein increasing the dynamics. This may be to emphasize power and control. The use of platforms, steps and ramps adds interest and variety.

The 'raked stage' is a slope that increases in height as you walk up-stage. It helps the audience see the acting area clearly. It gives added significance to an actor standing far up-stage. The level difference and its dynamics being above

Flown wall with perspex stained glass. Upper balcony and main stage set with canvas legs. Murder in the Cathedral. *Director: Zoe Hicks; Lighting: Jim Bowman.*

Interior scene suggested by a carpet, chairs, table and clock. Albert Herring. *Director: Thomas de Mallet Burgess; Lighting: Kevin Sleep. Guildhall School of Music and Drama.*

Flown painted gauze up-stage of flown cross and lectern for a centre-stage cameo scene. Actor David Shaw-Parker. Murder in the Cathedral. *Director: Zoe Hicks; Lighting: Jim Bowman.*

another area can be played out to good use. Stair units and ramps offer another dynamic. So too with ladders vertically set from floor to grid, balconies, and openings in flats indicating a level increase.

A wall with a gallery up-stage for chorus to look over gives scope to play

(Below) White card model. The centre door was the main focus as demanded by the play. The staircase was of particular significance. Dial M for Murder. **(See photo p.73.)**

on themes of judgement. A simple disk platform positioned centre-stage elevated only 0.300m immediately offers two very distinct spaces, one perhaps indoors, the other exterior.

A carpet and chairs imply a room, a blanket and hamper suggest a country picnic, a table richly adorned with banquet delights creates a feast, a floor-grate steaming evokes a prison or lower dungeon.

Additional variety is suggested through paint and texture treatments to different floor areas. One area may be smooth and shiny, another dry and coarse. Play up differences through contrasts. Groups of actors may remain within a visually defined area in silence while another group are in dialogue elsewhere. Adding separation to the acting area opens up the range of possibilities of movement and blocking for the director. This may encourage a more lyrical flow in the blocking.

Some plays may require more credulity. A thriller may be written with little or no flexibility for its plan. Dynamics concerning door positions, to furniture to sightlines may dictate the design. The murder may be so planned as to demand a particular layout.

Creating Focus

Organize the acting area in support of the characters, their immediate situation and free movement. Give characters appropriately stable ground relative to the situation. The floor is often a main focus for the audience.

The entrances to the acting area are of critical importance. An actor's entrance can be weakened substantially by a poorly positioned door. An entrance up-centre is powerful and dramatic. It is clearly visible to everyone and commands attention. A door centre-stage suddenly thrust open offers surprise and initiates drama. An entrance through the floor or from above is equally unexpected and draws immediate focus. A short squat doorway opening is significantly and characteristically different from a narrow slit that continues right up to the top of a monumental flat. Shape, size and position are the concerns.

The distance between entrance and on-stage furnishings needs careful calculating. A setting in isolation with a few pieces of furniture needs to relate to imaginary walls and entrance. Measure out distances between doors and furniture in reality. Of course a palatial home will have greater distances, the less grand the room potentially the less the distance. An isolated scene centre-stage may prove just too far from the side wings, the whole scene may need to shift to the side making the actor's entrance more relative. The longer the distance the more difficult to keep hold of the illusion. The audience may see it as an actor getting into position rather than a character moving about the space.

Stephan Loges and Nicholas Ransley keeping the focus to one side of a larger set.
The shop truck unit fitted into the rake stage-right, the wall hinged out to centre-
stage and was then set-dressed. Albert Herring. *Director: Thomas de Mallet Burgess;*
Lighting: Kevin Sleep. Guildhall School of Music and Drama. Photo: Roger Howard

Focus depends on the balance of the parts. All things have the appearance of weight. Scenic elements require balancing out with one another; the size of a wall to the size of carpet, or size of a bed to the size of a room. Elements become dominated by colour, texture, and light value. Scale very much plays a part here. And the more additions to the space there are, the more juggling to achieve a balance of the parts.

Always consider the dynamics of space with characters in motion. Look at diagonal routes across the stage for the actor. Always weigh out the odds for sustained focus within different areas. See to design supporting any point within the acting area as a good area for action. Support the extreme sides of the stage. If there is space an actor will be sure to use it.

Speaking characters are always the main focus. Costume design supports such character significance. The individual within the group is pronounced visually. Group situations often require the eye to focus on a few. Design relationships need to harmonize yet pay particular attention to individuals of importance. The use of visual accents achieves this along with values of characters being light or dark. The setting needs to consider these value differences. It needs to back up and help push forward the group and its individuals.

The set has to accommodate everyone on-stage. It needs to play host to varied moods and atmospheres. Settings need to keep an audience informed as well as interested. Black or white surrounds fatigue the eye after a short period of time. The lack of visual stimulation tires the senses. Too much visual play causes a kind of incomprehension and fatigue.

The Actor

The position of an actor in the acting area is crucial to the importance he commands. The design may offer an altered state and with it goes unique positions of significance. However, generally centre-stage and down-left and down-right are naturally preferred areas. Up-stage areas on the level stage are considered at times

Model with centre-stage the main focus. The scenic elements to left and right support the action to the sides. Shoemaker's Holiday. *Set Design: Debra Hanson; Open Stage Design: Tanya Moiseiwitsch. Stratford Festival.*

dead areas. Actors need to be seen to be heard. Lighting will draw focus onto a face. A face dramatically or simply well-lit will command attention. A face not drawing attention may prove to be too dimly lit, the strain for the audience in focusing causing them to lose interest. The actor's eyes and mouth draw focus. An actor with his back to an audience, even for a short period, will find himself inaudible. Things need to be heard and those saying them need to be seen clearly by all the house. The larger the theatre the more chance that up-stage positions will not favour even the best of vocal projections.

The actor needs to make two connections. One connection is to the other cast members in the scene since they are playing against one another. The second concerns reaching out to the audience. Both these connections need to happen concurrently. At the same time they are in action within the space, handling props, negotiating furniture and set levels, while wearing theatre costumes. They weave and interlock into a structured whole. The focus is ever shifting yet inextricably linked to the play's dialogue. The design should enable the actor to connect with the company and with the audience, in an ever-changing format of movement.

Movement

Actors may be required to accomplish great physical feats on-stage. And with it goes demands upon the set and costumes. A wall may need to offer up a wealth of opportunity – positions to perch from, with facilities to climb up upon, places to hide within, sections to break away or collapse, areas that illuminate, panels that revolve and doors that suddenly appear, segments hinged to open to reveal scenes set within. The surface may require drawing upon, be water-resistant, look aged and decayed, seem solid and secure but then suddenly disappear.

The stage floor will be of equal virtuosity. A surface might be used for dragging oneself and others across, have pits to descend into, pools of water to splash about in, sections to lift and rotate, be made of sand or grass or earth, be internally lit like stained glass, divide, separate and gush out hell's fires, change character from being a floor to becoming a wall, or lower itself down and totally seem to disappear.

There is no end to the demands on actors and the set. The convention of a wall remaining a wall seems too limited and narrow a perception.

Entrances and Exits

There are many alternatives for entering a space other than through a door. The director will go for the most effective and best possible solution. Dramatic value in an actor's presence is highly sought after. Until actors have left the stage completely, they are still very much an illusion of character and of significance. They command attention until they are gone.

To what and where are actors going when they leave the stage? It may be necessary for actors within a scene to appear to be coming and going to different places. It is not unusual for a set to have three entrances or more. The suggestion of space beyond must be as tangibly real as the on-stage set. With setting conventions on-stage it is necessary to respect the areas off-stage as seen through an entrance with the same sense of design.

Imagine a black box with a scenic wall positioned centre-stage, face on to the audience, running parallel with the back wall. In the centre is a large opening. Up-stage of the opening and to off-stage-right might be the entrance from outside. Up-stage of the opening to off-stage-left could then be to the hall. Down-stage of the opening and to off-stage-right might be a small room. Down-stage of the opening to off-stage-left could be to a larger room. Up-stage centre is part of a staircase leading to upstairs rooms. This simple set unit offers a fair choice of opportunity for direction.

SIGHTLINES

Approach design through working from the outside in. Consider the extreme dimensions that concern the whole space. Relate ideas of space and movement to the boundaries. Process architectural information down through to the centre-stage. Identity for the designed acting space establishes itself through processing information that concerns and relates to all six sides of the stage. These six sides stand together in direct relation to the auditorium.

All seats within the auditorium need to be considered. Of course it may not be easy to please everyone. However, what is visually presented on-stage should be in direct respect to their view. In no way is the outcome of designed acting space achieved without such respect to the surrounding sides and its elements. Nothing in, on and around the stage is in isolation. The six sides take the shape of: the back wall; two side walls; the floor; the ceiling; the dividing wall or the 'fourth wall'. An audience positions itself from individual viewpoints. Each view offers a standpoint from which they will perceive the play. Each view or angle of sightline presents a variable of visual composition. The framework of that composition must structurally lead the viewer's eye towards what is significant within each scene. The design must not only support the workings on- and off-stage, it must also successfully mask off any potential visual distraction.

Each side becomes a constituent part of the space and each makes its separate demand. The approach is to juggle the elements that concern the working and

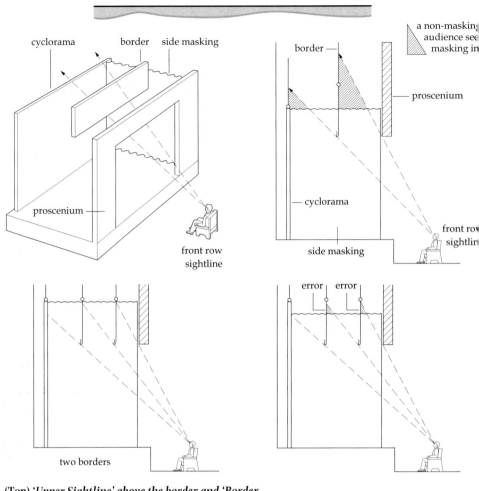

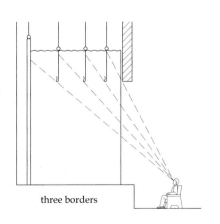

(Top) *'Upper Sightline' above the border and 'Border Sightline' beneath the border.*

(Top right) *Border and side masking creating an error. The grey area indicates the audience sees beyond into the ceiling or wings.*

(Above) *Perfect order, two borders side masking and cyclorama masking in harmony with no grey areas of error.*

(Above right) *The height of cyclorama and side masking are not in-line to mask properly.*

(Right) *Three borders enable the height of cyclorama and side masking to be shorter than with two borders.*

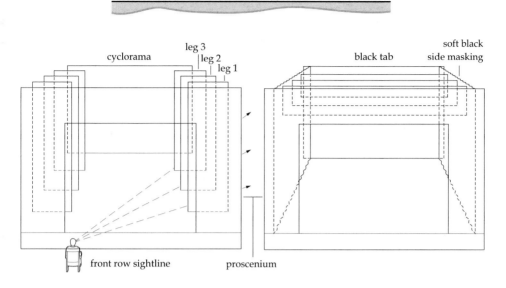

Side sightlines through the legs to the wings.

A Black-Box Theatre created with side masking, borders and up-stage tab.

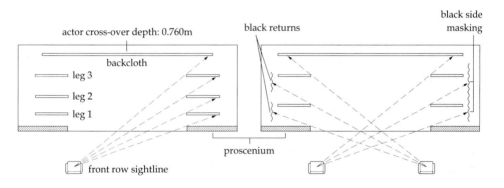

Three legs perfectly positioned to mask the wings.

Two legs with black soft returns or black side masking.

running of a production and to have it develop constructively and practically to 'fit' in harmony with the whole space. Design involves working concurrently with all expectations and demands from each side. Each theatre offers up variants in challenge or demand. Unusual considerations that might arise and should be taken into account are those of acoustics and air flow.

A stage having acoustic problems ultimately steers your design in favour of actor audibility. Actors need be heard. Although they have it within themselves technically to project clearly and audibly, they may need some additional help and support. A bare stage of considerable size may swallow up vocal audibility. At a certain point when travelling up-stage the voice may become distant or lost. Perhaps a delay in the voice reaching the uppermost seating is experienced. By presenting a mid-stage wall, face on, or a variation on this, one may avoid vocal sound from being lost up-stage. Angled scenery set on the sides may help broadcast sound outwards.

The back wall: A solid vertical plane meeting with side walls and grid above. This wall may have doorways through to dressing rooms or to the dock offering storage space. Rarely is this wall free of surface additions. The back wall might incorporate itself into part of the design, otherwise it may require total masking off.

Without a passageway beneath the stage, or behind the back wall, or one around the back of the auditorium, masking off the back wall may offer the only cross-over from side to side. The cross-over is an essential part of many a staged play.

Design that incorporates the back wall as part of the set may need to be treated. Not all theatres permit it to be painted nor to be built up onto to form relief. What the viewer sees of its height, especially from the front row of the pit, will affect your design decisions. *The two side walls*: The back wall may join with a curve to its side walls. Like the cyclorama that shapes itself into a horseshoe, so too do a few theatre spaces. Generally the side walls meet with corners to the back wall. The dimension from centre-stage to the side wall varies greatly. On the plan the measure from the on-stage edge of the proscenium to the side wall is the wing space. This is of critical importance, since the larger the space provided the less the potential constraint. Wing space both left and right of the proscenium may well differ.

The single purchase counterweight fly system will take up the full height and depth of the side wall. The double purchase system is reduced by half the height, leaving a clean wall from stage level to halfway up. Here, scenery has place to be stacked.

Keeping the wings at stage level clear for actors and travelling scenic units is no easy feat. Some lanterns may have to sit on the deck level, otherwise lantern ladders and booms may occupy space within the wings so as to light the show from the sides. There may be audio speakers in position here and special effects equipment, and with it a mass of cable. Step units or ramps down to stage level off the show level may obstruct.

Off-stage-right might be positioned the stage management desk with console and book. Any perch on the upstage side of the proscenium will house protruding equipment. Wing space soon becomes full of truck scenery, traversing and tracked scenery, property tables, a costume quick-change booth and costume-prop storage. The action back-stage in the wings can equal that on-stage, with stage management, the crew and dressers, all working to run the show, along with actors getting into position for their entrances. The access through to on-stage as well to back-stage requires careful negotiation here. On-stage doors may open to off-stage, actors and extras might be carrying off large awkward props that need a clear run off. Large groups or a chorus when exiting from on-stage should quickly disappear, with no bottleneck jams. There should seem to be from the audience's point of view a wealth of imaginary space beyond. Wing space is often never enough. Organizing and orchestrating within this space is an intricate part of design.

The ceiling: All seats within the pit or stalls take in a good view of the ceiling area above and beyond the acting area. The higher the ceiling, the more complex the problem. The fly tower should offer at the least the equivalent of stage height from stage level to the trim of the proscenium opening. Anything less will immediately restrict the height of scenic elements to be flown. The space above might house constructed scenic units, cloths on rollers or battens, sculpted properties and other constructed articles, a chandelier or ceiling fan, snow or leaf drop bags, harnessed actors, swings, rain- and mist-making equipment, and dozens of lanterns in many shapes and sizes. Set design ceilings when suspended from the grid generally require constructing to accommodate and facilitate some of the above being incorporated into the show, too.

All that the audience views through their individual sightline determines design's handling of masking. The masking off of all the elements within the ceiling is essential. What is viewed is considered part of the show. Its distracting nature, or intrusion upon the play needs to be controlled. The eye of the viewer should be continually directed to the speaking actor and their action.

The stage floor: An even floor is a justified request, both for the running and working of a show as well as for the actors. Actors can prove themselves brilliant at negotiating obstacles and step variations, and do so with a remarkable sense. The process of getting on and off the stage is, however, another matter. Having an entrance look natural and easy in terms of the scene's setting also means thinking through how the set extends itself offstage. Sudden shifts of level may interrupt the flow.

Truck units on the flat work best. On a ramp or slope they are somewhat uncontrollable. A track set within the stage or show floor may assist a unit's direct flow through to its required scene markings. Fixed direction wheels in the base will guide it along a determined path, however this is never foolproof. Small openings or slit panels within the show floor might interfere with shoe heels, as too might mesh floor panel inserts.

The floor may contain traps with stairs or steps down, carpet-cut traps that are sections that hinge open to accommodate carpet cloths being inserted and closed off to secure them in position. Most floors should take stage screws, those that do not become more demanding on design ingenuity. Designed show floors may house translucent light sections or panels, or traps for lantern spots. Holes offer smoke vents or pyrotechnic positions.

Bridges may act as lifts throughout a show for scene changes. This hydraulic system elevates sections running from left to right. Revolves set into the stage may also have hydraulic systems to lower a set to the under-stage.

The fourth wall: The proscenium is an obstacle. To many seats off the centre-line the view through is restricted. The wider out the seat, the more the view is of the wings on one side and less of the wing on the other. Seats in the gallery see less to nothing at all of the up-stage back wall and the up-stage floor. The wider the seats are set, the more their view may be distorted.

The opening is a frame or aperture. The audience peek in from differing angled positions. They will react to the play through how it is presented to them. What becomes removed from view to some does affect the way they appreciate or understand the play. The larger proscenium openings may not complement the play, a false proscenium of a hard or soft nature would better close down the aperture, yet it might create more of a complicated obstacle to view through to up-stage.

The principles of masking off a stage space from specific sightline positions are explained herein. The masking being proposed is the basic black cloth border and leg type. Variations on this through design can include painted cloths, cut-out, and constructed borders and legs. The basic aim and approach is to hide from view everything except the designed on-stage elements for the scene or act. Only that which is an integral part of the scene merits being in view.

The smaller venues and a restricted budget necessitate considerable compromise. In this case, a balance of the odds rules. Producing a stunning, bold design to distract the eye away from the school gym setting or hall, or incorporating a simple yet effective travelling backcloth that wraps round the set, would help narrow down the focus.

12

THE WHITE CARD MODEL, STORYBOARD AND MEETINGS

THE WHITE CARD MODEL

Have before you the renderings, collage work, sketches and freehand perspective drawings that represent your interpretations of the play so far. This model is developed with the same playful approach as the work already accomplished. The approach initially is to explore and discover. The concerns are for putting form to ideas. This will involve mass and volume, line, shape, scale, balance and composition. The approach should be adventurous and experimental.

Materials

Lightweight construction card and heavy paper
PVA glue
Scissors and cutting knife
Cutting mat, self-healing rubber type
Clear tape and masking tape
Scale ruler
Steel ruler
Triangle set-square
Pencils and eraser
White foamboard
Model-making wood or balsa
Small saw
Fine sandpaper
Soft wire, cutters and needle-nose pliers
Sculpting putty and plasticine
Light muslin or voile
Tissue paper
Kitchen foil
Sewing straight pins
Wood matchsticks and scalewood dowel

Most tools can be purchased through hobby, art and craft and hardware shops. The sketch models do not require sophisticated construction, nor a high degree of finish. This rough model is put together with ease. Changes should be

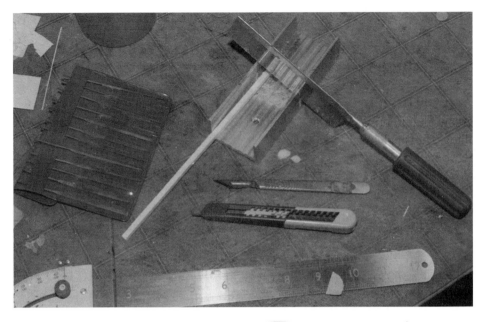

Model-making tools: cutting knives, saw and mitre block, steel rule, adjustable set-square and a set of files.

easy to carry out when necessary. The sketch model is a step towards the finished model. It is a valuable process in itself and good time should be given over to its development. It is presented unpainted.

Joining

Evenly apply a thin spread of PVA or wood glue onto both surfaces on the thicker card. This should be aired for thirty seconds prior to joining, giving the glue time to become tacky, which speeds up the drying time. One application of glue on the one surface may

NOTE

Keep glue with the cap on when not in use. Avoid leaving the glue lying on its side. Keep the nozzle clean. With contact adhesive and aerosol spray, work in a well-ventilated room. Read all instructions concerning tools, glues and sprays carefully. Manufacturing instructions must be respected. Store all tools, glues, cutting knives and potentially dangerous materials out of the reach of young children. Store out of sight if possible. Place all used cutting blades in a separate jar with a tight-fitting lid.

prove enough in most cases, especially on the thinner card. When gluing card to foamboard, the use of straight pins stuck through the card into the foam-board will help secure it in place while drying. Masking tape may serve to temporarily hold such joins in place. Clamp pieces together with small squeeze-sprung tweezers, or with clothes pegs. Allow glue to properly set before handling. Thin applications of glue on card dry rapidly.

The Scaled Figure

Construct a scaled-down replica of the human figure. Once constructed and placed in the model, all measurements make reference and relate to the actor. The figure adds a sense of realism. To visualize the life-size potential of a set, the figure is all important. Any questions concerning the size of a table, wall, door, chair, or the height of a window will then be relative to the figure. It is therefore essential to get certain proportions accurate.

Card

The simplest way to construct a figure is with card. First scale down the basic positions for head, shoulder, waist and knees. Draw in any costume details. A wash of colour will liven it up. Add a cut-out flat base of card or clear thin plastic. Give figures some gesture and expression for interest's sake.

Sketch model of thin card cut out and assembled in the model box, with scale figure. Wizard of Oz. *Polka Theatre.*

Epoxy and Wire

Twist a soft wire into an armature shape or skeleton. Apply over this a model epoxy putty. These two components when mixed harden in time. While curing, sculpt in the details using fine files. Once set, paint in flesh tones and costume colouring. Glue onto a flat, cut-out base of card or clear plastic. Note: epoxy putties may have instructions to wear plastic gloves. Read instructions prior to use.

Sculpting Putty

Use a sculpture putty that hardens with heat. Model the figure over a wire armature. Detail with fine tools and bake in the oven to dry. Follow instructions supplied for temperature and time.

Any further applications of detail to the figure should be done when totally dry. Tissue paper with PVA or wood glue, or paper paste used sparingly can create fine period dress detail. Build up three or four layers of tissue paper. Make several figures to represent actors of different height.

Set Construction Methods

Construction should challenge the eye by scale and formal spatial relations. Cut, paste, and tape together shapes and forms representing the structural concerns of your design. If you wish to investigate height, begin introducing simple geometric shape platforms. Add in walls and any suspended elements. Design the space using its width, depth

Figure with wire armature, tissue-paper, string, gesso primer and gouache paint work. By Evdokia Papadimitriou at Central St Martins.

and height. Introduce all your ideas into the theatre model box.

When introducing a wall, it may be an advantage to make two of different sizes. When several ideas arise, it is as well to present them both. Challenge ideas and seek out alternative solutions and approaches. Do not hold too firmly to one set idea.

Try to lift off ideas from the collage. Take suggestions of rhythm, pattern and movement and give them form and

(Above) *Oven-baked sculpture putty with metal armature.* Beowulf.

A finely sculptured putty figure designed and made by David Montgomery.

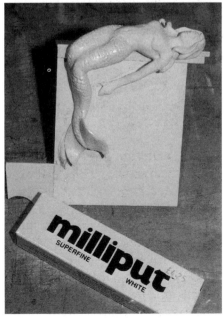

shape. Sculpt through the use of line. Alter the square model format to complement the curves. With weight bearing down on a scene interpret this into a suspended shape overhead. Introduce angled planes and/or organic forms. Approach the model as you approached the collage. Manipulate design elements and mould them into the shape three-dimensionally. Shift your angle of view to represent a front-row position.

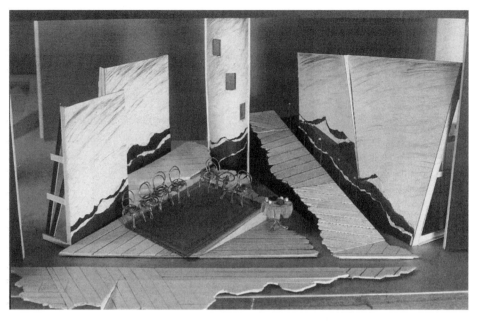

Unpainted model for Act I. Albert Herring.
Guildhall School of Music and Drama.

(Below) Sketch model units in fine card with pencil detailing. Shoemaker's Holiday.
Design: Debra Hanson. Stratford Festival.

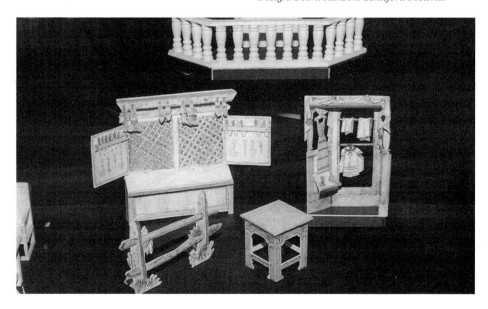

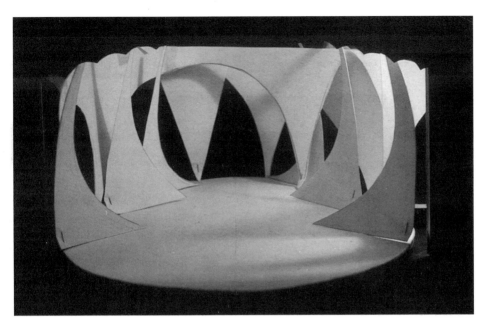

Sketch model, thin card set into model box with side lighting. Beowulf. *Polka Theatre.*

Simplify geometrically the shape of chairs, tables, platforms, beds, fireplaces and other such objects. Cut them out as simple cubes or squares and draw some detail onto the surface. Draw and measure up to scale and square off the sides. Adapt a throw-away approach. Quickly assemble a two-dimensional tree, try it for size. If it proves inappropriate, alter it or put it aside.

Sculpting with Light

Set up the model box with one or two anglepoise lamps. Test out your constructions thus far with directional light from above, from the side, through from the back or front-on. If desiring a less concrete suggestion of form it may be advisable to replace solid walls with gauze.

Muslin, voile and silk are appropriate for the scale model. They can be easily drawn on or washed with colour later on. If you want strong contrast with shadow, light projection may need to be somewhat limited. Later on an extra density of shadow can be obtained by effectively shading into the walls, flats, platforms and cloths. Cloths and gauze add illusion to space. Through their translucent qualities spatial depth can

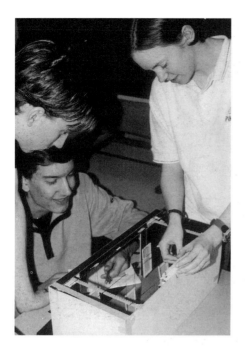

Students of RADA measuring up the design for plotting the flown unit positions. Gwen Thomson, Jon Rouse and Peter Harrison.

it to the stage. Break the audience into sections if the play wants breaking out of the confines of the proposed acting area. With traps to the under-stage consider action penetrating the stage floor. Add traps and openings to platform units.

Surface Detail

Surface texture in theatrical terms is a heightening effect. Every substance has a texture; when placed under intense multi-directional stage light, the effect of surface is greatly diminished. Consider the audience's distance from the set. Further away the surface becomes less visible. A heightening of surface quality gives it significance. The compromise is using alternative materials to suggest different textures. This moreover becomes an exceptionally interesting process of discovery.

Finding the appropriate material or fabric that simulates the original becomes something of an option. The factors that influence decision-making are: distance away of the audience, lighting levels, base or foundation material onto which texture will be built up, volume of surface and weight of material choice and degree of theatricality permitted before the result becomes an exaggeration of the truth.

Moulding details applied to a wall proportion it off. The divisions make the sections relative in scale to the size of the room and to furnishings. Architecture

become less tangible and more ethereal. An airy atmospheric quality may better be served by gauze. Consider carefully the material chosen and how it marries with and supports a particular idea. Frosted gel or clear plastic will bend and sculpt into creative planes. They offer a transparent or translucent quality.

Suspend and support scenery from wooden battens laid across the top of the model box. Avoid working directly onto the model box floor; instead place card over its surface. Challenge the auditorium through platforms linking

Scenic artist Karen P. Hay applying a latex and paint mix to black scrim
stretched over plastic sheeting. The texture of lace is enlarged significantly.
Three Sisters. *Design: Debra Hanson. Stratford Festival.*

such as windows, doors and fireplaces all require well-proportioned architrave detailing. The characteristics of architrave detailing vary from period to period. Its scale and elaborate nature is particular to historical period and necessitates some research. A small measure of 'proud' detailing enriches and adds visual interest.

The wall surface requires some thought and attention before detailing is applied. The canvas 'flat' offers an ideal surface, so too does a hard 'flat' with a canvas covering. Working into a primed flat is akin to an artist approaching a broad canvas. It is an inviting and highly desirable surface.

Add relief to model walls with card. Pay attention to the scale of card being applied. Suggest the door casing, skirting or baseboards, window framing, wood panelling, wall mouldings and fireplace mantle. Suggest thickness to walls, windows and doorways by putting in 'reveals' and 'returns'. These should be placed on any side of an opening that is in sightline.

Card scored through to half its thickness can then bend in two. Calculate and draw out the proposed thickness

Opposite page:
(Above) *Proud detailing applied to a fretwork screen.* Design: Neil Peter Jampolis. Banff Opera 1988.

(Below) *Scale model with architectural detailing.*

(Right) *Window unit detail with relief made lightweight with thick foamboard.* Three Sisters. Design: Debra Hanson. Stratford Festival.

Architecture mouldings and panelling. Model flown wall unit. Love for Love. Design: Stephanie Howard. Stratford Festival.

for returns then cut them out and score their corners. This saves gluing on return walls.

Make a wall more interesting with recess sections. Design in alcove recesses for bookshelves. If possible, include a bay window as opposed to the flat sash type. Such angled walls increase the structural stability of flats.

Brickwork can be quickly suggested by lightly scoring into the card with a knife. Repeat by scoring with a blunt-pointed instrument. This is to incise the surface to highlight the mortar lines.

Wooden floorboards, parquet flooring and exterior paving stones can be scored in the same way. Keep a dried-up fine-tipped ballpoint pen handy, this will work for the grooves.

Roof shingles and horizontal sideboard cladding to exterior walls can be cut from thin card. The overlapping quickly transforms the surface to life-like.

Basic kitchen foil draped and shaped becomes curtains, tablecloths and theatrical swaged dropcloths. Purchase the heavy duty foil. Paint up with gesso to white. Glued to a pole and sculpted, this makes a great flag blowing in the wind.

Modelling putty is suitable for sculpting into stone walls, carved grotesques,

Sketch model, thin card cut-out scenery and applied shingles and siding.
Wizard of Oz. *Polka Theatre.*

From modelled putty in the model to sculptured polystyrene walls on-stage.
Texture in strength of carving was determined by desired low-lighting levels.
Paul Boyle and Janet Bamford. Starlight Cloak. *Director: Vicky Ireland; Lighting:*
Neil Fraser. Polka Theatre. Photo: Roger Howard.

rocks, boulders and undulating ground formations. Model into the shapes avoiding detail, apply tissue paper overall with PVA. Build up several layers and allow to dry before applying gesso. When ready for handling it may be possible to pick out some of the soft putty from the base.

Texture into surfaces by thinly brushing out PVA and then sprinkling on sand, sugar, fine earth, or other granular substances.

For grass, use cotton velvet or flocking from a railway model shop.

Cork sheeting of a coarse type with a coat of gesso can look like an aged wall. Tear it through and piece it together to suggest cracks.

Foliage can be the real thing using a much finer version of the intended. It does dry and become brittle however. For the sketch model this may do. Alternatively, model shops sell shrub-like substances suitable for scale work. However, at this stage in model-making it is more important to hint at what you are considering.

Presentation model, foliage and texture applied to a garden truck unit. The fretwork and black portal were an initial proposal to reduce the truck dimensions. The Importance of Being Earnest. *Stratford Festival.*

THE STORYBOARD

A storyboard is presented through drawings. This reveals how the model might work with actors in movement. The format resembles stills or frames from a film, as a sequence. The view is the set front on. This is a quick way to test design for possible scene 'blocking'.

Focus on the actor and group composition within the proposed set. Draw up moments in sequence. Note a line or page for reference. Draw out the spatial relationships between actor and set and furnishings. This is especially useful when the setting is less than realistic. The drawings may highlight effects of lighting levels by placing groups in shadow or in strong cross light.

Add in alongside a plan view. Sketch this in without measurement. This

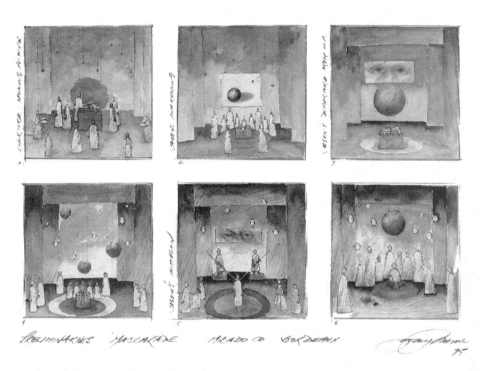

Storyboard. *Community Musical, France.*

clearly presents depth and width considerations. Animate the play through the storyboard. Work the play. Draw up moments of actor entrance and follow through illustrating their movement through to the next moment. Read a scene aloud and draw it up.

It is an advantage to photocopy your initial sketch representing the scene. Then draw the character and group positions in on top. Add in a wash of colour and some light to dark shading.

Work through the play depicting the more significant moments. Let this inform the design. This method of making design work for the play also proves of interest and insight for those involved in the production.

Measure and pace out for yourself proposed distances between objects. Read the play aloud and walk the distance from entrance to sofa. Try out the spatial relationships through a mock-up. Place chairs about a space and with your director act out the scene. Exercise the plan. Appreciate these concerns early on. Investigate alternatives in this situation and measure things out. Storyboard what you decide upon.

Transitions

Transitions are the timings between staged moments and scenes. Not always is it a scene change. It may be simply blocking the actors from the end of a scene into another. Transitions do not involve dialogue. The moment may require additional designing. It is most certainly about lighting changes.

A scene change may be done in black-out. This is not always appropriate for the flow of a play. How you shift and focus from scene to scene may become part of the concept. Transitions could be considered an essential aspect of design and blocking. The shift of mood and atmosphere from scene to scene may be the leading hand.

Perhaps you wish for a dream-like sequence for the scene change. Or, rather like a nightmare, the set and furnishings magically transform themselves into the new position. The sense of choreography can be as important for the actors as the furnishing and dressings. A gauze lowered down-stage of the action will soften the image, making it more illusory. A short strobe effect can enhance the expressionistic qualities. Scenery on the move without the bodies visible is both exciting and entertaining.

Transitions presented as part of the show complement the play's structure. Have design serve both these aspects. Consider them as part of the sketch model design process. Think of adding sound in terms of recorded

A 'fourth wall' show curtain designed with window unit insert. The scene up-stage was gradually lit to reveal Katija Dragojevic frozen in time prior to the scene commencing. Albert Herring. *Director: Thomas de Mallet Burgess; Lighting: Kevin Sleep. Guildhall School of Music and Drama. Photo: Roger Howard.*

noise and music. Let your imagination add to and influence these moments of change. Consider who might do the scene changes. With actors propose a plot of availability. If it is stage crew or stage management consider the look for clothing. An acting company as an ensemble may conveniently and most appropriately make all the changes, unless the set units are complicated by weight and scale. Perhaps you might decide to keep the whole acting company on-stage throughout the play, and have groups not in the scene prepare and set it up. A company may be kept on the sidelines during a scene. They may present themselves in groups, set alternatively to the side of the action. It may prove inappropriate for an actor to push on a truck or armchair and then immediately take on a speaking part. That actor may need to be in character while the change is ongoing.

Consider economizing by having extra space built onto a small truck platform with its wall, window and filing cabinet, to include the desk and chair too, with overflowing wastepaper basket as a pre-set. This speeds up any change and requires less hands.

Fade or dissolve a scene while the next scene is being set up. Overlap visually scene into scene. Or bring ongoing action down-stage and fade out up-stage for the scene change to happen.

Let transitions steer your decision-making process.

THE DIRECTOR AND THE MEETINGS

Meet with the director on a regular basis. Do not let your ideas develop too far along in isolation. Communicate and work collaboratively. Design needs a director. Successful design exhibits a strong relationship. It is essential that the director can make the design work. Ideas need to be presented with clarity. Listen carefully to all concerns and always take notes.

Be prepared for ideas not to be favoured. Aim to explain what has driven you into making decisions. Present back-up and all research that has initiated your work. Keep up a mutual understanding between you and the director throughout the process. Ask for ideas to be substantiated, as well as being prepared to back up yours.

How design develops depends very much on these discussions. Approach meetings with as open a mind as possible. Share the issues intuitively, intellectually and passionately. Enjoy the sense of occasion, make everything of being together. Talk about the play in every respect. Work jointly in the model box. Shape ideas into form together with the materials, scissors and tape. Present everything you sketch.

Meetings usually charge the designer up with many a new insight and approach. The meetings are loaded with opinion, viewpoint, and intentions. New thoughts need researching and interpreting. New set pieces need making.

Develop objective criticism of your own ideas and work. Present good arguments for your preferences. Keep an eye open for other ways of stating the obvious. Do not rush headlong into individual whims and flights of fantasy. Approach all suggestions with respect to what is already decided upon. Think things through carefully when introducing new demands.

THE PRESENTATION OF THE WHITE CARD MODEL

Work through the whole play, and include all set and furnishing elements. Represent all aspects with some form of mock-up. Do not paint out or elaborate on detail. Present the play as a package. Include a scale figure. Make sure there is a balance to scenes. Avoid too much emphasis too early on in the play. Build up design as the play builds up dramatically. Balance the play from the beginning to the end.

Be particularly interested in the opening moments – curtain up, lights up, the actor's initial line and dialogue are of essential concern. The first moments establish a lot for its audience. Plot the start of the play. Plot the working of scene changes and transitions.

Define the approach and potential numbers for who moves what.

The white card model should be accompanied by a rough ground plan for each scene. This presentation to the theatre is important for many reasons. The meeting will largely concern the overall play and the intended aim through the concept adopted. There will be considerable interest over the internal workings.

A point to remember here is that this is a working model, representing ideas in progress. You are not required to have all the answers. The meeting should initiate discussion concerning problems and how they will be resolved. Such problems are to be tackled together. Expect criticism. Present the research. Explain and express your intentions clearly. Present yourself with having an objective viewpoint.

The meeting may involve those from production. These may include, besides the director, the production manager and/or technical director, the lighting designer and stage management. Others could be from carpentry, wardrobe, properties and sound departments.

Each department presents their concerns. Issues may involve the theatre repertory, budget, staff and labour, the build dates, on-stage workings, storage and the run. It is a good time to enquire into the capabilities of the department. Establish their ability to facilitate the realization of the design. This may initiate the need to contract out of house for some making. Be prepared to propose preferences for material, with regard to construction. The clearer you can be, the more concrete will be the final picture for preliminary costing. Describe the intended look for surface and texture. The department's expertise may suggest a material you had not considered. When in doubt, ask for costings on several materials.

There is generally time after this presentation for unresolved problems to be investigated. What first appears as negative feedback may in time become constructive. Expect and welcome criticism. The first meeting will raise many issues. Note them and work them through later with the director.

An Approach to Problem Solving

Example

The director David William requests that a stuffed crocodile jumps out of the closet. Ask what is the intended effect? Investigate what the surprise aims to achieve. Which moment and what aspect of his character is to be affected? What effect should this have on the audience? If there is no context in the play's dialogue how should it be timed, to what specific moment? How shall it be got rid of and by whom?

The character is an aged eccentric astrologer and severe hypochondriac. He surrounds himself with charts, instruments, potions, charms and mystic nonsense. His closet, from which David wished the crocodile to spring, was already set-dressed and furnished appropriately.

The designer Stephanie Howard believed there to be several problems with this request. The effect and impact on the audience would be short-lived. The object would come springing out and be on stage level in no time. It would attract most of the attention when on the floor, distracting the eye from the actor's reaction. The actor picking it up to put it away would look weak and, if he knew his home well, why his surprise at this in the first place?

After considerable thought it was reinterpreted and proposed by Stephanie that a human skeleton be cabled and rigged to come out with the action of the door opening. It was more appropriately positioned, more in keeping with his other collectibles, and made him all the more ridiculous by showing his forgetfulness. The skeleton retracted back with the door closing. The solution was equal to the intention, yet better complemented the moment and character.

Example

Approach a technical problem through the simplest conceivable solution. Avoid over-complicating. Imagine achieving the intended effect by the most elementary means. If you were to construct a working model, how might the scaled-down version become mechanically animated? Think of toys and how simple

Finished model outside its model box, with down-stage-left animated garden.
A Patchwork Quilt. *Polka Theatre.*

systems serve to animate an object. Research into the mechanics of toys.

A growing garden was produced by using flexible rods inserted into hosing. The hose was fixed at one end to the base of the earth structure, the other ends were fixed to a wood panel in an off-stage position. The flexible rod had foliage and flowers fixed to one end. The inside of the hose required oiling. Stage management off-stage pushed the appropriate rod on cue and delivered the surprise. It had charm through its simplicity. Some flowers were detachable enabling the actor to pick them.

There was also a vine growing up a trellis that produced runner beans. Loop cables were fixed round two rollers, one at the top, the other at the base of the trellis. Attached to half the cable was a vine. The roller was turned from an off-stage position from behind the trellis. Beans grew out through tubes set within the trellis by the same method as the flowers. They were picked from the vine. With a run of over seventy performances the demands were for a foolproof system.

Example

In *The Knight of the Burning Pestle* a character was without an available actor. 'Dwarf George' had only a few lines, not a substantial part. Luckily he was always in the company of 'Squire Tim'. A puppet was proposed by director Bernard Hopkins. 'Squire Tim' spoke the puppet's lines. As they were knights, opportunity arose for George to become more representational of the period. He was put on horseback and decorated with heraldic emblems. A playful solution was found that complemented the comedy.

Actor Geoff McBride with 'Dwarf George' the marionette. The Knight of the Burning Pestle. *Director: Bernard Hopkins; Lighting: Kevin Fraser. Courtesy of the Stratford Festival Archives, 1990. Photo: David Cooper.*

If at all possible use the other side of a constructed unit. Give it a new and different life. A 'periactus' is prism-shaped, offering up three sides. A whole set can truck and in a moment be rotated to become another scene. Incorporate reversible truck units into walls. Once repositioned they reveal alternative architectural details. A fireplace might become a cupboard unit, with the mirror above rotating to a bookshelf unit. A portal opening within a wall may have internal sliding doors. Panels may revolve to produce a change of interior furnishing. Boxes may flip over on the top side to produce fixed set dressing for a scene. Floor traps may open to bring forth monsters from the deep. Trapdoors within a wall allow for surprise entrances. Walls may fly to reveal an inner chamber. A whole new scene may unfold like a pop-up book through hinged double doors opening outward. A wall may crack in two then traverse apart revealing a paradise. Flying-in a flat with additional cable fixed to its base edge can be thereby raised up into a ceiling unit. With swagged fabric attached, a setting is quickly established.

Adam Sunderland sorting out the trap in which the dragon will be housed.
Beowulf. *Polka Theatre.*

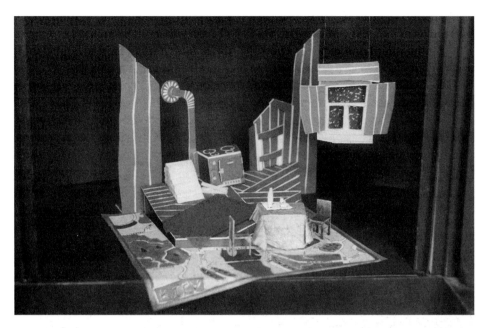

Hansel and Gretel *sketch model showing interior scene. Flown window, truck walls, stove, log pile and hinged ramp in table-top position and floorcloth. Pop-Up Theatre.*

Example

A platform stage or raked floor constructed specifically for a production offers up great opportunity. Various shaped traps and panels can hinge either up or down. Introduced to such a raked stage in *Hansel and Gretel* were many such surprises. The initial interior setting included a wood-burning stove and pile of logs. The log pile remained in the outdoor scenes. The stove hinged to the rake edge and flipped back to an up-stage-off-stage position, its underneath side then became level with the rake. For the open fire out-of-doors, a panel in its base rotated to reveal the wood fire from inside. Smoke was pumped through the wood from beneath the stage. The gingerbread house was first seen with a trap rising at centre to form a triangular window unit. Light from below attracted the eye downwards. A panel from within the stove rose to reveal the chimney and more smoke was emitted. The top of the log pile rose up to become the door, and through the hollow pile of logs was the passage down to the underground house. With an interval change the interior was set.

(**Above**) Hansel and Gretel *exterior scene with truck trees, gate, trap window, trap chimney and ground row.*

Hansel and Gretel *underground interior with above-ground window flown with ceiling, wall drop and side masking. Trap oven and ramp cage.*

Down inside we see high above the exterior window – structurally part of a ceiling-wall unit. The centre-stage trap was replaced with a triangular unit, now the oven with hinged glass door. Out of this shone red flickering light and smoke circulated within. Another trap revealed a caged structure.

The Revolve

The revolve is a disk platform built within a floor framework. Fixed directional wheels rotate beneath. The revolve is manually operated from an off-stage position. The revolve facilitates easy transitions and scene changes. Even small-scale revolves can prove an exciting feature. The revolve has power to surprise, for it is capable of carrying on whole new settings with actors already in place. It encourages graceful transitions. An actor walking a revolve in motion suggests the passage of time. They may enter into a scene from another that is disappearing.

Dividing the revolve into half or several wedge-shaped pieces, creates

Small-scale touring set with up-stage and side masking cloths. Free-standing leaf-shape trees are canvas laced onto steel frames. Floorcloth and centre-stage a revolve platform. Cuckoo Time. *Directors: Jane Wolfson and Michael Dalton; Lighting: Steve Allsop. Pop-Up Theatre.*

False proscenium with truck unit and apron extension. Act II on reverse of truck. Lettice and Lovage. *Director: D. Michael Dobbin; Lighting: Linda Babins. Alberta Theatre Projects. Photo: Trudie Lee.*

opportunity for several set locations. Add a false proscenium that meets with the circumference, aligning with walls built onto the revolve and the focus is within that section alone. A set in the off-stage position can be reset and dressed. The main problem is noise off-stage as the revolve is like a drum. Portable masking units must be placed off-stage of door openings to suggest rooms and space beyond.

A small-scale revolve may be operated by being wound up with cord. A castor platform with a wooden lid could be so constructed with a section between for a sash cord to wind up round. Pulling the sash from an off up-stage position will rotate it. A simple yet effective device.

The False Proscenium

Good reasons steer design into reducing the acting area. Costs may well be a priority. Another reason may be to achieve a cameo scene across an expansive stage. The structure may welcome being animated with trap panels, hidden doors, internal illumination, or open itself out to puppetry portals. The framework could be made to be climbed upon and lived in. The false proscenium may require side masking through to the wings. Try altering its angle to put a slant on the play. Apply bold ideas to this opportune set unit.

Cloths and Tracking

Creating a sense of illusory depth within a small space comes though using scenic gauze, cloths and the cyclorama. Theatrical suppliers offer large scale flameproof fabrics suitable for on-stage use.

Classifications

Non-Durably Flame Retardant
A fabric that has been chemically treated with a soluble solution. After a long period of use or once cleaned these require reproofing.

Durably Flame Retardant
These fabrics are chemically treated so as to withstand a number of cleanings before reproofing is necessary.

Inherently Flame Retardant
These fabrics are naturally flame retardant, due to the construction of the fibre.

Ruth Finn and Simon Doe taking a break from spraying two drop gauzes. The paint frame lowers through a narrow slit in the floor to the basement level at the push of a button. Beowulf. *Elms Lester Studios.*

Materials most commonly used:

Front Tab	*Velour*
Front Tab Valance	*Velour*
Legs	*Bolton Twill, Wool Serge, Velour*
Borders	*Bolton Twill, Wool Serge, Velour*
Tabs (on-stage)	*Bolton Twill, Wool Serge, Velour*
Cyclorama	*Matting Duck, Filled Cloth, PVC*
Back Drop	*Calico, Canvas*

Drawing and watercolour rendering for a country village 'ground row'. Construction of thin plywood, built in a zig-zag. *Drawing and Rendering: Gary Thorne; Design concept: Neil Peter Jampolis. Banff Opera, 1988.*

Cyclorama

A cyclorama can curve itself around the acting area on three sides or be simply set up-stage as a drop cloth. Allow space for lighting either at front or back, depending on the type of cloth. Some are front projection only, others front and rear. Discuss with the lighting designer appropriate distances required in respect of floor lighting on the down-stage floor level. Such lights require masking off on the down-stage side. This may invite a ground-row with a cut-out silhouette. Perhaps a townscape or landscape becomes appropriate.

A cyclorama illuminates the space with a wall of light. The wall can become richly coloured and brilliantly illuminated. Projected moving cloud

A cyclorama with projected transparencies. The soft focus gives the impression of distance. One of four plays running in repertoire. Hunter of Peace. *Director: D. Michael Dobbin; Lighting: Harry Frehner. Alberta Theatre Projects. Photo: Trudie Lee.*

formations are attractive illusions. Slide images project to create pictures. Suspending a gauze down-stage of the cyclorama will soften the wall effect. This soft focus offers up a less tangible surface, one with more illusory depth. Clouds then projected onto the gauze create greater illusions.

Scenery and set units down-stage of the cyclorama require close inspection for gaps allowing the bright light to filter through. The outer shape of such scenery should be interestingly designed. Alter the amount of cyclorama visible to the audience by introducing variable solid cloths and cut-out set units down-stage for variety.

Scenic Gauze: A mesh of a lightweight material and weave. Use as a softening

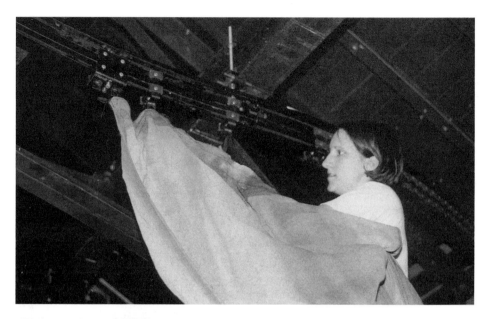

(Above) *Leonie Bass tying off a gauze to a curved tracking unit. The curtain was hand-drawn across the stage by an actor and pulled off-stage by stage management in the wings.* Beowulf. *Polka Theatre.*

A sharkstooth scrim with dye boldly run down its surface. This curtain set the scene for the interior of the cave. Beowulf.

effect and to create greater illusions of depth. With a lit cyclorama set at a distance up-stage of a lit scenic gauze, the painted image on a gauze appears with more spatial depth. A scenic gauze is painted with dye so as not to fill the mesh.

Sharkstooth Scrim: A more densely woven material mesh that offers more scope when intending to make something appear and disappear magically. When lit only from in front and above, the cloth appears solid, making anything up-stage invisible. Lighting from the front as well as lighting anything up-stage of the scrim produces the illusion of painted image and object merging together. With up-stage lighting only the painted image disappears completely. Excellent for transformation effects. The paint needs to be dye so as to not fill the mesh.

Bobinette: This open-weave material offers a more softening effect than the scenic gauze. It may find use as a illusory soft divide when set near the proscenium. The lit scene up-stage will appear distant through this veiling. Even within an intimate theatre the effect produces a divide that does not visually interfere but rather adds to the sense of the ethereal or its distance. It softens the hard-edged reality removing it to a stage further away.

Gauze, scrim and bobinette are available in white, grey and black. They are supplied in very large widths suitable for wide stages. Back-painting lightly over in black on a grey or white front-painted gauze reduces the bounce and misty quality when back-lit.

Gauze takes well to appliqué. Apply foliage and textural detail and also paint in to blend with the material. Remember when back-lit the untreated gauze will disappear. Cut the profile edge to complement the design. Hang as borders and legs. This may produce a forest or glade with great illusory depth.

Cloth may be painted to achieve the same effects. Apply surface detail as in canvas leaves, string or yarn for stems, and paint. Rubber latex thickened with paint and squeezed through a bottle adds dimension to stem and branches. Cut out the profile and hollow out sections to make them see-through. Apply gauze to the backside to keep unsupported sections and flaps from becoming limp.

Curtain Tracking, Tripping and Rollers

The traverse curtain is in two parts, dividing at the centre. They overlap at the centre for full concealment. Theatrical suppliers carry a range of tracks from lightweight up to heavy duty to support heavyweight cloths. The draw pulley system or handline is operated from a position off-stage. The hand-drawn or walk-along type is without a pulley system. The tracking can be assembled to form a straight or curved single track.

Tripping a cloth involves folding a cloth back on itself. With limited height above the acting area this approach proves advantageous. A batten across the top of the cloth is cable suspended through pulleys. Drawing the line from off-stage raises the batten to the ceiling. The remaining visible cloth needs

The banners were flown out to half their height as the ceiling is a dormer pitch. The remainder was flown out through tripping the cloth. Two banners and a heraldic cloth over the feast table set the scene for inside the Court. Starlight Cloak. *Director: Vicky Ireland; Lighting: Neil Fraser. Polka Theatre. Photo: Roger Howard.*

tripping out. An additional batten is attached horizontally on the up-stage side of the cloth. This batten's position is determined by the restriction of flown-space and drop-cloth dimensions. The batten has a cable and pulley to help raise it up behind the first batten. A longer drop cloth may require several battens attached to trip it out.

Roller drops can operate by the single fixed roller that lowers a cloth in effect like a roller blind. The roller's fixed position above unrolls through a handline off-stage. Alternatively, the roller is attached to the base of the cloth. The roller extends a short distance beyond the edge of the cloth on either side. The cloth top edge is fixed to a batten that is secured above the stage. The cloth is first rolled up to the raised position. Cables that run through pulleys attached to the top batten are attached to the roller ends. The un-rolling motion of the cloth while it lowers causes the cable to wrap round the roller ends on either side. Drawing in the cable from off-stage causes the cable to unwind which causes the roller to roll-up the cloth. Having a cloth unroll itself in a downward direction, with the roller positioned on the up-stage side of the cloth gives place to a painted image on the cloth appearing to unfold magically before one's eyes. The image appears from top to bottom. This is opposed to a drop cloth being lowered in from above with the bottom of the painted image appearing first and revealing itself from bottom to top.

Lengths or runners of cloth may be suspended to stage level to set a scene. They may first appear by a quick-release mechanism that lowers them in. Along the top edge of the cloth are rings sewn on at intervals. Attached to a batten that is fixed in the grid are more rings set at intervals between the rings on the cloth. A cable is laced through these two sets of rings and left dangling loose at one end. The other cable end leads through to off-stage. When someone pulls the cable out through the rings the cloth drops to the floor. With height to the grid, attach the batten to the cable through pulleys so it may be lowered for resetting. Instead of the rings and cable, velcro on the cloth and on the batten will produce the same effect when someone on-stage pulls the cloth.

With a raked or platform stage and false proscenium a black tab may be pre-set beneath a thin hinged trap running the width of the stage. The batten or fly bar to which the tab is attached has a cable at each end that runs up to the grid as a line set. With the trap positioned just up-stage of the false proscenium the bar ends and the cable will be masked from sight. On cue the tab is raised from the floor upwards. Using a black tab facilitates a hidden scene change once it reaches a certain height. The tab continues to fill the stage with black. With good timing the tab base flies out to reveal the scene change completed. This is quite an unusual effect.

Strings of fairy lights attached to the up-stage side of a black gauze or tab, with the bulbs poked through and lit in darkness, produces the glorious effect of a starlit night. A property-costume may take on the same treatment giving a character celestial significance.

Walls

Flats are timber frame constructions with canvas or hardboard coverings. Hard flats have canvas applied with glue to offer a more ideal surface to paint into as well as to hide board seams. Flats are braced off-stage. An adjustable length brace is angled and fixed to the stage level by weights or stage screws, the other end being hooked through a ring attached to the flat back.

Off-stage of a flat, with bracing, stage weights and stage screws to the floor. Property dressing tables for the actors. Guildhall School of Music and Drama.

(Below) *Wood flat showing back view, 'plate' triangle.*

Canvas stretcher flats are somewhat vulnerable when touring. They require careful storage, anything leaning against the canvas indents and stretches it out of shape. The most ideal covering is heavyweight cotton duck. Lighter weight cotton ducks and flax canvas are also available.

Canvas flats can produce seemingly solid walls. Doors, when slammed, unfortunately cause wobble in the canvas. This may steer you to build hard flats. Canvas flats take texturing as long as it is with a flexible binding agent. Walls with windows and fireplaces can be of the canvas stretcher type. Doors may swing open when a flat is not braced to true vertical. A door may be incorporated into the bracing of a flat, by being fixed open at an angle.

Floor Cloths

Many a theatre's floor is a major focus for its audience. Floor cloths effectively transform a black space into a

Metallic gold powder in a glaze medium decorate the walls in a written manner. The once white carpet is transformed through stencil work and hand painting. The Importance of Being Earnest. *Director: David William; Lighting: John Munroe. Courtesy of the Stratford Festival Archives, 1993.*

designed space. Design may also be applied to hardboard sheeting, vinyl flooring, wood planking and metal. Many theatres permit their floor to be painted.

A canvas floor cloth rolls up and tours easily. It wears extremely well, and transforms many a sad surface. Cloths may be painted and/or textured. Applications of paint should be kept thin to avoid build-up that cracks.

Rostrum base-unit framework, shown stored on their sides.

Painted cloths can suggest any surface and material. They may resemble stone paving, cobbled streets, parquet, wood planking, marble, mosaic, parched arid earth, or have a fantastic bold pattern. Changing a floor design between scenes is possible using a cloth.

When touring, applying latex to the back of the cloth will prevent it slipping. Some venues do not allow the cloth to be taped down at the edges. Alternatively, a commercially available non-slip netting is suitable. Latex-backed cloths must be rolled up so that the back does not come into contact with itself. Latex acts like contact adhesive, once dry it will stick to itself.

A white carpet may be transformed into a rich decorated effect by hand painting. The paint needs to be a dye of a permanent kind. Stencils may assist in repeat patterns.

Platforms

Consider floor levels, platforms and raked flooring, even for touring productions. A collapsible wood rostrum is ideal. There are steel units commercially available with plywood tops. These platform units offer corner slots for inserting aluminium legs. This scaffold tubing is inexpensive and lightweight. The raked stage may be constructed this way. The legs are cut to different lengths at either end. Many theatres keep a stock of solid deck platforms.

13

THE PRESENTATION MODEL AND DRAWING

THE PRESENTATION MODEL

The quality of model-making should reach its peak with the finished presentational model. The intended aim when choosing the material for the model is to

Author with presentational model. Beowulf. *Polka Theatre. Photo: Roman Stefanski.*

suggest as much as is possible. Many of the materials used in the sketch model apply. Other techniques and materials now stand to better complement design. This model represents accurately surface

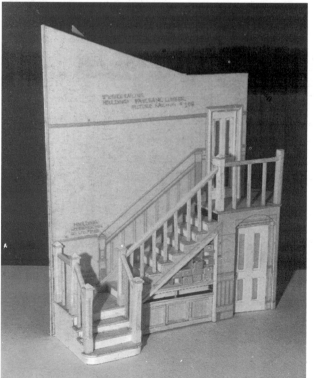

Finished model with set dressing in detail. The full model made from card. Dial M for Murder. *Grand Theatre, Canada.*

(Left) *Apply dye-line copy from technicals to card with spray adhesive. Cut out and build up three-dimensionally from the elevation.* Design: Neil Peter Jampolis; Model Maker: Gary Thorne. Banff, 1988.

texture and colour. Metal, wood, plastic and card are favoured construction materials.

Carpenters do not build directly from measuring up the model. They refer to it for many of their queries. The scenic art department will exhaust the model as a reference. If it is not built to withstand a lot of handling, it will soon look quite worn.

There are commercially available materials to suit the scale model. Fine fretwork, sheeting, mesh, rod, dowel and tubing can be bought in brass, aluminium, fine-gauge steel and plastic. A large assortment of coloured,

patterned, reflective and decorative papers are readily available.

Shops selling scale railways offer foliage and shrub materials, fine grade sand, gravel and stone. They sell scale brick or stone-pressed sheeting. Look for grass sheeting or flocking in various colours. Scale figures prove expensive, yet with smaller scales as in 1:50 it may be easier to buy some in.

A few model shops cater specifically for the architectural model. Fine pressed detailing in wood moulding can be found in strip lengths. This, however, can be made up from scratch with a little ingenuity and patience.

Model unit measured out in elevation before drawing up on the actual construction. Guildhall School of Music and Drama.

Wood, foamex plastic and paper. *Model Maker and Design: David Neat.*

You are not required to buy expensive materials for model-making. Yet good tools are a great investment. Bead and jewellery craft shops are excellent for small-scale bits and pieces. Sprays and paints are on offer in a wide range of finishes.

Wood glue, PVA, preferably fast drying, two-part epoxy resin glue.
Cyanoacrylate glue, and the accelerator: available in three consistencies.

TOOLS AND ADDITIONAL MATERIALS FOR MODEL-MAKING

Cutting tools, scalpel, matt knife, fine hand-saw.
Cutting mat, self-healing type.

CAUTION

Cyanoacrylate glue bonds skin and eyes in seconds. It requires adequate ventilation since the vapours are harmful, and it must be kept away from heat and flame. Keep out of reach of children. Always read thoroughly the directions for use and the safety instructions before using.

Foamex plastics, styrene plastics, clear, white, or grey. Available in sheets of variable thickness, rod, tube, and dowel.

Brass sheeting, fretwork, rod, tube, dowel.

NOTE

The choice of brass is for its easy-to-solder characteristics. It cuts with ease, takes little heating up to solder, holds well together, is lightweight and most effective for scale work.

Soldering iron suitable for brass, flux and coil.

Pliers, small clamps, sprung tweezers

Piano wire, a very rigid strong wire in various gauges; note: it will not solder.

Model paints, both spray and liquid, primer sprays, black matt spray.

Spray adhesive, the craft type for paper and card.

Compasses, steel rules, set-squares, calculator.

Gesso, a water-based white primer.

Modelling putty oven-dried and air-dried, sculpting epoxy compounds.

Scale rules, metric 1:25 (1cm = 25cm), 1:50 (1cm = 50cm) are the most commonly used.

Sandpaper and fine files.

Turpentine or white spirit, methylated spirit.

TECHNIQUES AND APPROACHES

Wood

Look at 0.8mm–1mm-thick model-making wood sheeting. It is available in hard and softwoods. Suitable for panelling, planking, roofing, siding and flooring. Easy to cut and score. Glue onto a card base to avoid any warping. Avoid getting wood glue on any part of the top surface, as this would repel any water-based paint and ink. Measure accurately the spacing between planks, and avoid exaggerating. Sand lightly to unify if necessary. Texture into wood by pressing coarse, hard material into it like mesh or sandpaper and scratch into the surface with fine tools. Apply washes of water-based colour or ink. Build up colour gradually. It is difficult to remove stains of colour. Shade into the cracks when necessary. Rub graphite and charcoal dust gently over the wood to age. If a gloss finish is desired, finish with wax polish, or methylated-based varnish. This will not affect the water-based properties.

When intending to paint a wood-like finish on-stage, choose to work with card rather than wood. Prime with gesso and dry-brush colour over gently to simulate the grain. Paint mouldings and proud detailing prior to gluing to the finished walls. Use hardwood sheets and wooden rod and dowel for tables, chairs and furniture units.

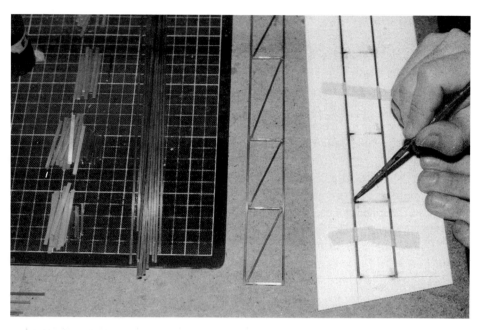

Designer David Neat systematically laying out the parts for unit construction.
To be soldered after taping down to the elevation.

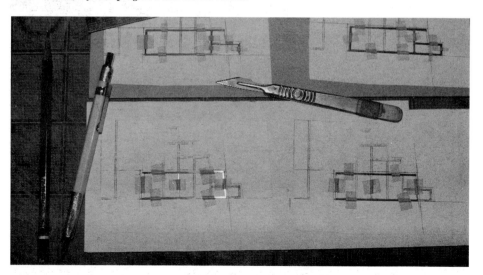

Photocopied elevations with brass rod pieces taped into position prior to
soldering together.

Metalwork

Any metalwork that features in the design may need to be made with brass. Fine 1–2mm square or round rod is ideal. The intended cut can first be scored with firm pressure using a cutting blade. Score all round the intended cut, then snap clean in two. Measure accurately when cutting.

It is a good idea to draw the structure to scale in the form of an elevation for each side of the unit. Cut the brass and tape it onto the elevation. Leave the joints free from tape. Butt the joints close together. Lay out the whole elevation, then move on to soldering it.

Apply a light brush of 'flux' to the joints before soldering. With a hot iron either apply a small amount of solder to the tip of the iron and then hold it to the brass joint till the solder runs into the joint, or hold the iron to the joint till the brass is hot then touch down the solder. A small amount will do.

When joining two already soldered units, take care not to overheat them as this may cause what is already joined to come apart.

Plastics

Foamex is a fine porous plastic sold in sheets. It is available at 1mm thickness

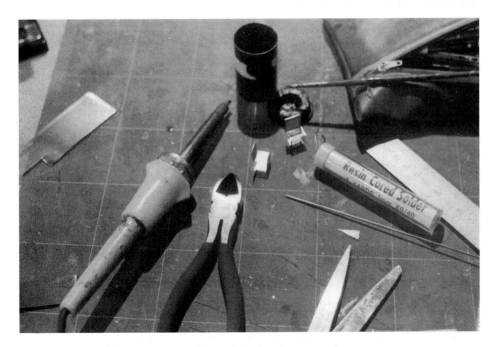

Soldering gun, solder, wire cutters, flux and fine brush on a cutting mat.

Foamex plastic cut and applied to brass-soldered framework. Atlanta Duffy model making for designer Alison Chitty.

(Below) *Heavy Idenden compound spread coarsely over the surface of a flat, with base colour already mixed in.*

at its thinnest. It is not a cheap material, yet it is a delight to handle. It moulds and shapes beautifully with heat, and cuts with ease. Once primed it paints up brilliantly. For texture to be applied requires the plastic to be coarsely sanded first. The glue is cyanoacrylate and an accelerator is necessary to speed the drying to within a second. *See*: Cautionary notes in the material list. When joining, simply apply a very thin spread of glue to one part, press the parts together immediately and add a drop of accelerator with a fine watercolour brush. Apply the accelerator near to the glue so it runs to the glue. Do not touch the brush tip to the glue or it will dry instantly into the glue; any glue in the bristle will harden and destroy the brush. Never allow the glue to come in contact with your skin, otherwise it will instantly bond it to whatever it is touching.

The glue fuses the edges together. To break it apart after joining would cause a break not necessarily to the joint. Once you get the hang of handling this glue, the results are clear, precise and very strong.

Styrene is a dense harder plastic, not porous. It is more brittle, and less easy to cut. It is available in a wide range of tubing, rods, dowels, sheets. It can be found as clear, white or sometimes grey. It bonds with the same glue. The selection of rods, dowels, tubes and small plank lengths come in various thicknesses, the smallest being 0.075×0.075m-square lengths.

Textured Surfaces

Gesso is a fine acrylic primer suitable for base-coating card, sanded plastic, wood, and fine fabric such as voile or silk. Combining with fine grits will boost the texture. Household polyfiller pre-mixed offers a coarse texture finish, for stone, brick, coarse plasterwork and stucco finishes. It will bond well if the surface is first sanded. Too liquid a nature causes warping to card. Always test a sample first. It may be necessary

Plaster compound used as texture. Two samples of brick both with plasterwork, one has sawdust scattered over and pressed in, the other is simply textured by dabbing.

to reinforce the unit from behind. Small set furnishings and properties can be creatively assembled from jewellery bits and pieces. Be adventurous and invent; with gesso and paint the transformation can be spectacular.

Painting

Give the model the exact look desired. Age in with shading, shadow, breakdown and distress to create a unified look. Treat the model as if it were a painted picture. Harmonize the parts to give emphasis overall. Blend in colour and let colour merge. Unify the floor with the furniture, the furniture with the wall so that no one part draws focus.

Tighten up the picture by keeping to a restricted palette. Let colour layer itself on the surface, avoid flat blocks of one hue. Let colour mingle and brushwork show. Keep working the whole picture from the viewpoint of the audience.

To create a fine splatter use a toothbrush or an artist's mouth sprayer. Stipple colour over colour using a bristle brush. To glaze a water-based paint, use methylated bases, varnish or polishing wax. On metal finishes apply colour with French enamel varnish. This is a transparent paint. Mist gentle sprays onto coloured surfaces to give increased surface depth and textured looks. Air-spray inks onto any surface. Add theatricality to the model by

Finished model with painted show curtain. Search for Signs of Intelligent Life in the Universe. *Alberta Theatre Projects.*

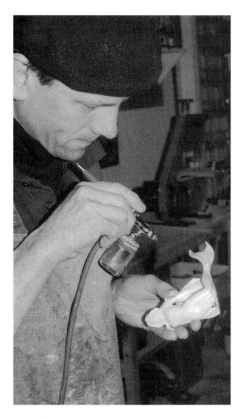

Model maker and designer David Montgomery applying colour through an air-spray gun.

battens, securely fixed with glue. Note the fly bar number on the batten for aligning with the bar numbers set out on the model box. Aim to present the set model exactly as you wish to see it on-stage. Be particular to detail.

PERSPECTIVE DRAWING

Exercise

You will need several sheets of A3 lightweight drawing or tracing paper. Pencils 4H, 2H, H. Eraser and erasing shield. Pencil sharpener. T-square, drawing-board surface, set-square, scale ruler at 1:50 or 1:25.

One-Point Perspective

As you look off into the distance, lines that run parallel appear closer together the further away they go. Railway tracks provide a simple example. The lines converge towards a vanishing point. This vanishing point sits on a horizontal horizon line called eye level. A cube viewed through one-point per-spective shows its sides drawn converg-ing to this vanishing point on the horizon line. Perspective presents it as it would actually appear to us. This form of drawing is easily understood. When we look at objects in space or at build-ings positioned alongside one another

heightening its sense of dimension and illusory quality.

Present the model complete with masking borders and legs. Scenes in-volving large groupings of furniture and dressing might want the parts fixing to a thin clear plastic sheet that fits nice-ly into the model in one go. Suspend all overhead items with fine wire to wooden

on a street, the vertical lines appear closer together as they recede, the horizontal lines appear angled or sloped.

One-point perspective is effective for the viewer positioned front on. For any other stage type, other than the proscenium, this fails to work. On the thrust or in-the-round, this perspective would simply look confusing. Too extreme a perspective and an actor in the up-stage position will look larger than they should in scale to architectural detail. Perspective requires a raked floor. All architrave detail will have sloping horizontals. With seating set wide to the proscenium, those to the sides will view perspective as extreme and exaggerated. The above also applies to two-point perspective.

Two-Point Perspective Drawing

Take a sheet of paper and draw a vertical line up through the centre. Two-thirds up the page draw in a horizontal to represent the horizon line. Near the left edge of the paper mark a point on the horizon line. Call this vanishing point one, VP1. Place a point on the centre vertical one-third up from the bottom of the page. Label this 'A'. At about centre of the vertical make a dot and call it 'B'. Draw in construction lines joining VP1 to both A and B. On the horizon line between the centre vertical and the right edge of the paper place dot VP2. With construction lines

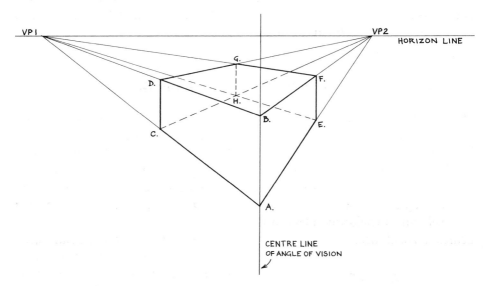

Two-point perspective. A view looking down upon the object from above. Two vanishing points on horizon line. Note the vertical centre line of angle of vision.

join VP2 to A and B. On line A–VP1 place a dot at the half-way point, call this C. Draw up a vertical line from point C. Where it joins with B–VP1, call this D. Between A and VP2 make a dot and label it E. Draw up a vertical and where it joins B–VP2 call it F. With construction lines join: D–VP2; F–VP1. Where these two lines cross label as G. With a dotted line draw a vertical down from G; this will stop at the point where E–VP1 and C–VP2 cross each other. Label this H. Draw a dotted line in for H–C and another for H–E. The view of this perspective drawing is looking down upon the object from above.

If you could take A–B, keeping it the same distance apart, and slide it up the centre vertical line with the converging lines remaining attached to the vanishing points, you would obtain two other significant views.

The Street Eye-Level View

This would appear when the line A–B is divided in half or below half, by the horizon line. This means that you would not see the top or bottom of the object you are viewing. Imagine this object to represent a building and your eye level comes to half-way or less up its nearest vertical edge.

View From Below

Now imagine that you can shift A–B up the vertical so that A is positioned above the horizon line. With the converging lines diminishing to their respective vanishing points the view is now looking up to the object from below. The eye level is positioned below the horizon line and therefore beneath the object.

Sets with perspective create problems for doors and windows. Slope-edged window units may become rather troublesome when required to open. The same is effectively true of doors on a rake. The problem with doors is which vertical you hinge them from, and which way they swing. Doors may require their bottom edge cut to an angle, not in line with the perspective. A door hinging open towards off-stage with its bottom edge in line with the rake requires the off-stage platform to be parallel to the theatre deck.

From Ground Plan to Perspective

Ground Line: (*See* illustration p.180.) The distance estimated between the eye level and the ground plane level on which the object sits. This is an estimated measurement and with practice in drawing up the Three Views, this will make sense.

When looking down upon an object, the point for the ground line is positioned below the eye level (horizon line). To view an object from below, the point for the ground line is positioned above the eye level.

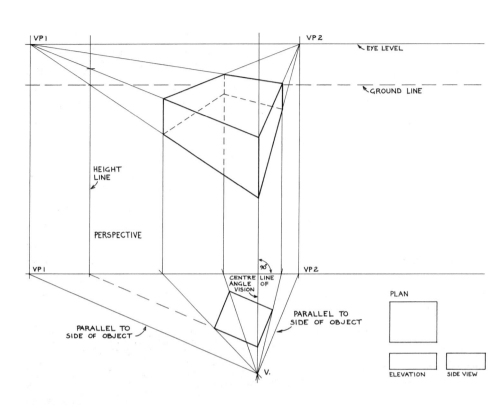

From ground plan into perspective. A view looking down upon the object from above. Note that the measurement up the height line from the ground line is depicting the actual scaled size of the object's elevation height.

Take the plan. Decide upon a position for the vertical line that indicates the eye of the viewer (angle of vision). On this vertical line indicate the viewer position as point V. As with the previous example the vision line falls in line with the object's nearest vertical edge. Now establish the 'picture plane'. This imaginary vertical plane will have the object, in perspective, drawn upon it. A horizontal line, drawn perpendicular to the viewer line, indicates the base edge of our picture plane. From point V draw in lines that are parallel to the object sides. These construction lines meet the picture plane and produce the vanishing points VP1 and VP2. On the plan draw in a projection (dashed) line that continues one edge of the object through to the picture plane. From this point draw in a vertical line perpendicular to VP1–VP2. This is the 'height line'. The elevation of the picture plane is established by drawing vertical lines up from VP1 and VP2. Knowing that we want 'a view from above', looking down on the object, draw in a horizontal eye-level line some distance up from the picture plane. This allows space for the perspective drawing between two horizontal lines, positioning the object below and not above the eye-level line. Now label appropriately the points carried up VP1 and VP2.

Establish for yourself the distance between your eye and the ground plane for the object. Imagine a section view of yourself standing before the object.

Imagine that your eye view encompasses 180 degrees, a half-circle, from below to above. Draw a line from the eye to the base of the object and, where it meets on the circumference, draw in a horizontal line. The distance from your eye to this plane is the estimate wanted.

This estimated distance is indicated on the height line down from eye level. At this point draw in a horizontal 'ground line'. Using the same measured scale as the ground plan, measure up the height line from the ground line, the elevation height of the object. From VP1 draw a line connecting with

One point perspective design. The vanishing point to which the lines converge is up-stage centre. *Designer: Stephanie Howard; Director: David William. Stratford Festival.*

this point and beyond to meet with the viewer line. From VP1 draw a line connecting with the point, where the ground line meets the height line, carry it beyond to meet with the viewer line. From VP2 draw two lines through to meet with these points on the viewer line.

Take lines from V to pass through the corners of the object on the plan, on to the picture plane base. From these points along the picture plane draw up verticals. Where they meet the converging lines, they establish the object's vertical sides. From these points converging lines are drawn to VP1 and VP2.

Perspective drawings just as easily depict interior and exterior settings.

View perspective drawings by artists and architects. Theatre design often shows the use of perspective. There is always a theatrical slant however, rather than pure perspective displayed. This is due to the nature of the stage to its audience and effect desired.

Viewing a building, in perspective on street level, establishes eye level running through the object. We are facing it head on. It is noted, in normal practice, that eyelevel sits 1.6m above the ground-level line. With smaller buildings, a lesser measurement is preferred, at 1m above the ground-level line.

Both technically produced and freehand perspective drawings can be greatly enhanced with shading, representing

Freehand perspective drawing for The Linden Tree. *Arts Educational Drama School* **(see photo p.50).**

light direction and shadow. Add texture to heighten natural relationships. Perspective drawings achieve a semipictorial view. They take on very real impressions with colour washes.

Sophie Leach with charcoal drawing stick scaling up from the model. Guildhall School of Music and Drama.

SCENIC PAINTING MATERIALS AND TECHNIQUES

After applying primer to a flat, draw out the design first using charcoal; for large walls place the charcoal into the end of a length of bamboo or simply tape to the end of a stick.

Scaling up: Take the original rendering and lay over and tape on a sheet of clear acetate. Draw off a grid measured into squares using a chinagraph crayon or permanent felt-tip. On the wall or canvas draw out a scaled-up version of the grid in charcoal. Draw in all major lines of the design. Then begin painting in washes of colour.

Projecting an Image: Take a colour transparency of the original rendering or image and with a slide projector enlarge the image directly onto the flat or canvas. Use an overhead projection for smaller work. Photocopy onto A4 acetate. Project and copy out significant details.

Theatre Paints: These are available as a concentrate. They are expensive, yet they go a long way due to their strength. They dilute into washes yet stay intense in colour. There are an excellent range of colours available.

Glaze: A translucent acrylic varnish, water-based. Used as a seal or as a tint

(Above) *Scaling up, grid lines on acetate in preparation for enlarging.*

(Left) *Linda Rodrigues painting in shadowing on the columns. She holds the original as a reference.*
Designer: Neil Peter Jampolis. Banff Opera, 1988.

(Above) *Use an overhead projector to draw up onto the canvas. The image needs to be photocopied on acetate.* Designer and Assistant: Madeline Herbert and Maxine Foo. Guildhall School of Music and Drama.

(Right) *Compressed air-spray gun working onto a gauze stretched out on a paint frame. Ruth Finn wearing a respiratory mask.* Elms Lester Studios.

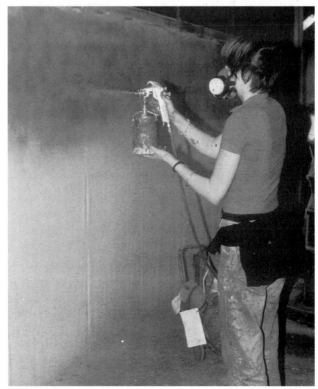

by mixing with colour pigment or paint. A strong acrylic varnish can be used on hard flooring to protect the painted surface from being marked. Available in matt, satin or gloss. Work over colour to create a colour layering effect.

French Enamel Varnish: A shellac-based dye mixture diluted using methylated spirit. It dries to a hard, durable transparent glaze. Can be applied to materials including metal and fibre-glass. Used in property and costume painting. A good range of saturated colours.

Stipple: To finely texture a look of stone or rusted metal, first prime, then brush on a base colour, dip a flat wide bristle brush into paint of a darker shade and dab the tip onto the surface. Another darker colour lightly stippled over adds more depth of texture. The second colour could be stippled using a rough sea sponge for coarser effect. Glaze over with an acrylic varnish to blend and add spatial depth.

Use the stipple effect to add shadow; keep a bucket of clean water alongside and soften the outer edges of the shadow by wetting the brush, shake out the excess and dab into the wet surface of paint.

To add interest to a flat block of colour, lightly stipple over a shade lighter or darker of the top coat. Any layering of paint effectively adds to the dimensional qualities.

Anna Barnett stippling with a brush and adding texture with a foam roller. Guildhall School of Music and Drama.

Flogging: To create bolder stone effects and coarser linear-type texturing. Fix to a dowel end a dozen 30cm long strips of cotton canvas, minimum 0.03m wide, dip into paint, wring out excess and flog the wall surface varying the angle or direction to build up the texture. Vary the shades of colour as you layer.

Cross-Hatch: Layer fine drawn lines like an etching. Use a wide bristle brush,

Flogging with cloths dipped in paint.

dip only the tips of the bristle into the paint and brush off the excess before very lightly brushing across the surface. Brush out a stroke, let dry and do the same over top, the second time changing the direction of the stroke at least 45 degrees. A brush with string wrapped round the heel and through its bristles separates the bristles effectively. Use two pots of colour and blend as you go for a coarse effect. The technique of dry-brushing is essentially that of applying one stroke that creates a set of fine lightly drawn parallel lines.

Rag Roll: A softened crushed velvet look. Brush or roll over the wall with the base-coat colour, dip a cloth into paint a colour shade darker and wring out excess. Use rubber gloves. Crunch together the cloth into a roll shape, start at the top of the wall and rest the cloth against it, roll the cloth downwards gently with no real pressure. Work in a true vertical direction. Overlap the edges of the pattern. Alternatively, attach a twisted cloth to a paint roller wrapping it round in a twist from one end to the other. Use a paint roller tray and roll out the colour.

Scumbling: This creates a coarse circular plastered texture. Using an old wide bristle brush, dip into the paint and holding it perpendicular to the surface press the bristles down onto the surface so the bristles bend, then twist or rotate the handle and lift off. Create these quarter-circle shapes going in every direction, letting them overlap at the edges. Use a lightly textured paint for additional relief.

Splatter: A breakdown effect giving a pitted look, that when finely done could simply shade or blend things together. Use for highlighting into surface using metallic or complementary colours. Thin paint with water to a runny consistency. Use a wide soft long-bristle 6–8in 'laying-in' brush. This is used for applying the base colour to large walls. Dip in paint and flick gently, or tap your brush hand against your other arm.

Drawing with a stencil onto gauze for a repeat pattern. Ruth Finn. Polka Theatre.

Stencils: Create a repeat pattern using a cut-out stencil. Use a sharp blade. Stencil card is waterproof so as not to warp. Apply colour with a sponge, roller, brush, spray or cloth. For a multi-repeat pattern to be produced on a large scale it is advisable to place holes in the stencil at points to indicate registration, then 'pounce' through with powder of chalk or charcoal, aligning the stencil to these marks for the next repeat.

Roller Effects: Foam rollers can achieve a repeat pattern when a design is cut out of the foam. This suits finer patterns. A pattern of striped lines, fine leaves, diamond shapes, checkerboard effect, or fine- to coarse-pitted pattern can easily and cheaply be achieved. Try wrapping string or yarn crudely round the foam and other woolly type rollers.

Wood Grain: Rubber wood-grain tools are commercially available and with these a good range of effect is achievable. They cost little and when cared for last forever. The art is in getting the paint to the appropriate consistency

Duncan Clark and Stuart Tucker applying brick texture through a wood stencil. Guildhall School of Music and Drama.

(Below) *Scenic artists' textured foam rollers.*

(Above) *Wood-grain samples and rubber tools.*

(Below) *Samples showing base board colour and cracked effect using a heat gun.*
Guildhall School of Music and Drama.

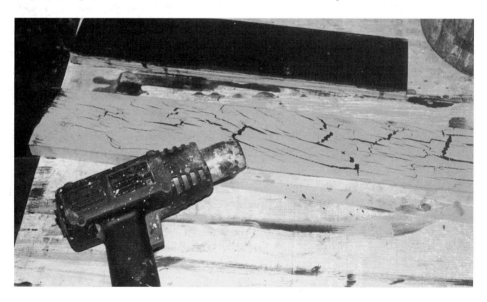

and achieving the right twist of the tool to produce the grain.

Use the dry-brush technique with different brushes and the effects of grain can be made to look quite real. Look very closely at the intended grain of the wood you are copying and make allowance for enlarged scale.

Remember that wood panelling wants to visually recede as you go back in depth, so all top 'proud' surfaces want to be lighter than the background panels.

Cracked Paint: Brush out a dark base wood colour and when dry apply a coat of hot 'size'; let dry completely then paint over the top coat colour and while this is drying blow over with an electric heat gun. This causes a shrinking in the size, so that the top coat separates with crack lines. The thicker the application of size the more severe the cracking effect. It may be advisable to varnish over later with a strong acrylic glaze to protect the surface.

Breakdown and Ageing: Use spray paint, splatter effect, dry-brush, air-spray and stippling effect. Blend in and fade out shading and shadowing. Let it merge

Cracked paint effect and breakdown on perspex window corners.
Guildhall School of Music and Drama.

Sample board of foam wadding and crunched paper dipped in hot size, showing possible textures for foliage hedgerow. Guildhall School of Music and Drama.

gently from the light to dark. With a brightly lit set the breakdown will have to be more subtle than with a set that has dark lighting levels.

Size and Dyes: Pigment dyes are generally mixed into a medium called 'size' then painted out. The size is sold as a crystal and requires soaking for 24 hours in water. See instructions for the ratio. Once soaked it is heated in a double boiler. Place the pigment into a container and add a small amount of size to cover and stir in well, then add the remaining size to dilute. Pigment in size dries many times lighter than how it appears as mixed. Dye on canvas-covered flats can be back-lit to produce great effects.

Stained Glass: Take fine bookbinding linen and stretch out and attach evenly to a cut-out frame. Black in the leaded lines with paint or use black all-weather sealant for windows. Let dry and paint using dye. Alternatively take Plexiglas or Perspex and leaden the lines in the same way. Lay the sheet

Plywood fretwork with steel framework. Covered with crumpled tissue paper. Sealed with PVA. Primed, painted and highlighted with metallic powder in glaze. The Comedy of Errors. *Designer: Patrick Clark. Stratford Festival.*

(Below) *Wood table with plaster face, plasticine detailing and vacuum-formed plastic appliqué, in preparation for scrim covering and fibre-glass treatment.* The Comedy of Errors. *Designer: Patrick Clark. Stratford Festival.*

horizontal and apply French enamel varnish generously to the areas.

Tapestry: Take very coarse hessian and with dye paint out the design. Apply some dimensional highlights using textured paint, or stitch heavy yarn through in parts before applying dye.

Metalwork: Wood fretwork can be turned to metal by first applying crumpled tissue paper with PVA layered over several times, keeping a surface irregularity. Seal over with more

Polystyrene with paper template attached. Pinprick holes have charcoal 'pounced' through for detail transferring. Designer: Patrick Clark. Stratford Festival.

diluted PVA. Paint out the base dark-metal colour and when dry, dry-brush over a lighter metal shade. Then high-light by dry brushing over lightly with metallic silver or gold powder mixed with glaze.

Vacuum Formed Scenery: This is a thin plastic sheeting that has been heat-shaped over a relief; it is a half round impression. Available in architectural mouldings, architraves, panelling, columns and their capitals, stone, brick, book-ends, and much more. It can be painted and easily stapled to wooden base-boards.

Sculpture: Carve out of polystyrene and cover by applying either muslin, scrim, or parcel wrapping paper with PVA. For sturdy work, cover with a fibre-glass and resin coat. Paint to the finish required.

Metallic Finishes: Powder metallic is available in a good range of silver and golds. They mix with glaze mediums as a binder. With gloss glaze the finish is highly reflective.

Carved foam with muslin applied using PVA.

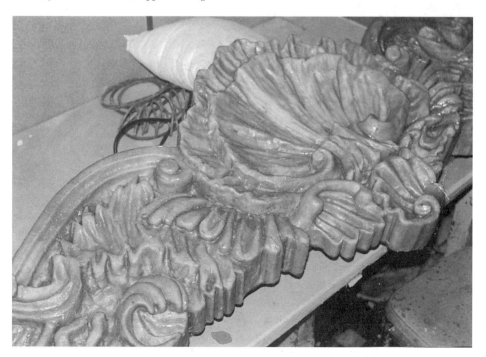

Fibreglass covering over the muslin skin. Designer: Patrick Clark. Stratford Festival.

GLOSSARIES

ART AND DESIGN GLOSSARY

abstract form created by artists, separated from matter, not concrete. As rearranged or organized for artistic purposes.

accent emphasis or attention given to elements within a composition. Can be created by light, contrast, scale.

aesthetic concerned with and sensitive to art and beauty.

amorphous without form, shapeless and unorganized.

architectonic implies characteristics of sound architectural design. Involving stability, strength, constructive organization, formality.

assemblage work that is an organization of miscellaneous parts, with found material. Related to collage, junk art, ready-made. Pertaining to three-dimensional bas-relief type formats.

asymmetrical that which is without symmetry.

automatism applies to a technique in drawing, writing and painting, where reason, conscious control of thought are eliminated. Allows for unconscious images, emotion to express itself. A stream of unconsciousness, or automatic writing.

balance feeling of equality in weight, an equilibrium of the various visual elements.

bas-relief carved design which projects out from the background to which it is attached.

biomorphic shapes shapes irregular in form, resembling freely developed curves in organic life.

chiaroscuro of Italian origin, using light and shade in order to achieve a three-dimensional effect.

chroma the quality of saturation or measure of the colour content. Spectrum hues are of maximum saturation. Chroma colours are the hues and their derivatives formed by intermixing.

collage application of found materials, keeping within a two-dimensional surface format.

colour temperature of warm or cool characteristics. Those colours with close relations on the colour wheel to orange are considered hot, while those most adjacent to blue are cool.

composition the organization of all the elements of a work into a unified whole.

contrast a combination of opposite or nearly opposite qualities.

contour a line following the edge of the surface of an object. A line identifying form and shape with sensitivity to its variety and true characteristics.

craftsmanship aptitude, skill or manual dexterity in the use of tools and materials.

cubism a school of painting and drawing with attention to basic planar components of what we see, studies taken from all viewpoints and thereafter assembled to recreate a totality by such a juxtaposition.

curvilinear stressing the use of curved lines.

decorative quality emphasizing the two-dimensional nature of any visual elements, which, when applied, enrich a surface without denying the essential flatness of its nature.

design the art of relating and unifying contrasting elements, structural and compositional, towards a form to create interest and order.

distortion any change made by the artist in size, position, or general character of form that differs from the way it is normally perceived by the eye.

dynamic tension where line creates direction, the eye attributes it with the quality of movement. Linear tension is created to deflect the eye from concentration at any one point.

eclectic showing the use of developed ideas and style as taken from various sources. Of differing tastes and styles.

elements the basic design components of line, colour, shape, texture, value.

expressionism pertaining to art that is related to what is felt rather than reasoned or perceived.

fantasy a departure from accepted appearances and relationships, for the sake of psychological expression, dreams or the unconscious.

figure and ground the enclosed surface tends to become the figure, while the enclosing one will be ground.

foreshortening showing a contracted view, of what would appear as projected in full extension, therefore not giving a fully characteristic image as seen; a change in the proportions to imply near and far through contracted form.

form the structure and content of visual patterns that make up a representation of objects. The arrangement of visual elements that go to produce a harmonious whole.

formal an orderly system of organization.

format the shape and size of a composition, or the basic overall ordering of forms within a composition.

frottage literally rubbing, suggesting the three-dimensional through a tactile textured surface, produced by rubbing over with medium.

illusion imitation of the three-dimensional visual reality as created on paper or a flat surface of the picture plane, through the use of perspective, directional lighting, etc.

illustration a narrative art, usually commercial, with a story to tell, with subject matter as important as the aesthetics.

impasto a built-up layer of paint.

impressionism painting that achieves a general effect without detail, an effect capturing the immediate sensations of light values and colour values.

integrate to unify and make into a whole.

linear made through use of line.

linear perspective consisting of conventions dealing with the progression of planes to a horizon, with a system of linear depiction of the three-dimensional.

local colour a tone which takes its colour from nature, from the actual in nature.

mass a distinct shape or form which has weight and emphasis due to size, colour, value contrast, texture, linear definition, etc.

medium (media, pl.) any materials used for expression in art and design. Also the substance mixed with pigment to form a fluid suitable for application artistically.

modelling the use of value, tone, light and dark to depict illuminated volumes and solids.

monochromatic colour chords consisting of the same hue, but of different values and chromas.

monolith a large single block or mass.

motif the main theme, subject or repeat within design.

multiple imagery device used to create sense of surprise or unease, in which a form appears as one thing at first glance then becomes something else.

mural a wall painting.

narrative that which tells a story.

naturalism a style of form essentially descriptive by representing things visually experienced, without personal interpretation or expression.

plane surface that wholly contains every straight line joining any two points within it.

positive shape the enclosed area representing the initial selection, they may suggest recognizable objects or as planned non-representational shapes.

proportion in the arts, a designed relationship of measurements.

realism a style in which the basic impression of usual reality is retained.

relief limited three-dimensional masses bound to a parent surface.

rhythm a continuous flow that is accomplished by repetition of regulated visual units, the use of measured accents.

romanticism a style developed characteristic of a point of view that extols spontaneity of expression, intuitive imagination, strong emotion, subjective attitude.

shape an area having specific character defined by outline, by contrast of colour, value, or texture with a surrounding area. Shapes act as planes in relation to others, receding and advancing or moving in one way against another; they occupy position within the spatial context.

simultaneous contrast the direct contact between two colours tends to reduce the similarities and intensify the differences of the colours.

subjective the personal opposed to impersonal.

symbolic forms having meaning, through culture, tradition, or collective, a form or character that represents something applied. May represent idea, situation, not the thing itself but rather a sign of the thing.

symmetrical tensions that exist on sides of the actual centre, a balance formally from side to side, top to bottom.

tactile referring to a sense of touch.

technique the manner and skill with which the artist employs his tools and materials to achieve a given effect.

tint mixture of colour with white, or a thin transparent wash of colour or stain.

tone the quality of brightness as in light and dark.

transition steps or scale, a sequence in which the adjoining parts are similar or harmonious.

translucent allowing light to pass through, yet diffusing it so that objects seen through it cannot be clearly distinguished.

transparent transmitting light rays allowing for things to be seen clearly through.

trompe l'oeil a painting technique that creates a strong illusion of reality. The viewer may not at first realize that it is a representation.

vanishing point the points to which the sides of a three-dimensional object could be drawn if extended into infinity or to the horizon. Vanishing points appear on our line of vision, on the horizon or eye level.

virtual image an image seen that has no substance, no tangible existence.

volume term used to describe the three-dimensional quality of a form.

THEATRE GLOSSARY

act drop the front curtain.

acting area the space wherein the actors act.

alternative theatre refers to the space or the style of presentation in acting. Alternative refers to an experimental approach.

angle flat a flat used as a buttress or return for another flat.

apron stage extension level with the deck that breaks through the proscenium, extending towards the audience.

architrave the moulding for door openings and windows. Seen as applied wood, carved polystyrene or as a painted effect.

arena acting area totally or partially surrounded by audience.

ASM assistant stage manager

auditorium the space beyond the acting area for the audience

backcloth or backdrop a wide stretched cloth attached to a batten at the top, covering the width of the stage. Fixed at its base to the floor or with a length of steel rod inserted within a sewn base pocket. With painted effect whether it be landscape, townscape, sky or other.

backing the scenery set behind an opening, window, fireplace or door.

back-stage all that area surrounding the acting area up-stage of the prosce- nium. May include workshops, dress- ing rooms, offices.

bar or barrel the pipe of steel sus- pended by cable to which scenery and lighting are attached.

batten a length of wood to which a cloth, made taut, is attached top and bottom.

batten-out a wood length to which flats are attached for flying as French flats.

black-out opening on a black-out means that the curtain goes up on an unlit scene. When stage management calls for a black-out all lights are turned off.

block a pulley containing lines for fly- ing scenery.

blocking the arrangement of move- ment by the actor with the director.

book flat flats hinged so that they fold together.

boom a vertical bar for lighting.

border vertically hung hard or soft panels attached to bars suspended above the stage generally positioned with their bottom edge in line with the top of the proscenium. Either plain or designed borders mask the ceiling above a set, restricting the view of lights and flown scenery.

box set a three-walled set, the fourth wall removed for the audience to see in.

brace a wood arm angled to support the back of scenery. Attached to the stage level with a stage-weight or with stage screws.

brace cleat the attachment at the back of a flat to which the brace is hooked.

brail a rope used to pull scenery in a direction from where it naturally hangs. Attached to the end of the fly bar.

breast to pull a bar up or down-stage so as to reposition flown scenery from its natural vertical.

ceiling piece the scenery unit which sits on the top of flats to form a ceiling.

centre-line the exact centre position of the stage, a line running between down-stage and up-stage.

cleat the metal hook attachments fixed on flats to which a thrown-line is secured then fixed, so to secure flats together on-stage.

cloth a scenic canvas drop hanging vertically.

counterweights the system for rais- ing and lowering scenery. Scenery weight is balanced by counterweights.

cradle housing for the counterweights.

cross-over the way across stage from

left to right, and right to left, not in view of the audience.

cue a signal for change, used to initiate an actor entrance, change scenery, etc.

cut-cloth a canvas cloth with cutaway sections for doorways, or the contour edge cut round painted canvas foliage. With intricate cut-cloths a netting may act as fill-in to help keep its shape when flown vertical.

cut-out flat a shaped or designed contour edge flat.

cyclorama a plain cloth or hard wall to serve as backing for the acting area, lit from behind or from in front. May wrap or curve itself round along the sides.

dead the correct height for scenery, flats, legs, borders, cloths to hang. Their raised or on-stage positions.

dock the storage area.

dolly a truck unit with wheels.

double purchase the counterweight system that has the cradle travel half the distance the bar travels, and is designed to leave the side wall of the stage under the fly galleries clear of flying equipment.

down-stage the acting area nearest the audience.

draperies soft curtains used often to replace hard scenery.

draw line the pull line to operate a curtain on track, to traverse the cloth in and out.

dress parade an opportunity to see all costumes with actors, not necessarily on-stage.

dressing the decorative elements that furnish a set design.

dress rehearsal the on-stage rehearsal involving scenery, furnishings, lighting and costumes. There are several prior to opening night.

drift the length of suspension cable between the counterweight bar and the top of the piece to be flown.

drop a suspended cloth, on a roller or flown.

DSM deputy stage manager.

edge-up to make upright and make vertical a piece of scenery onto its edge.

elevation the view in a drawing that shows verticals and their planes.

entrance the process of, or the place for, entering the acting area.

exit the process of, or the place for, leaving the acting area.

false proscenium a frame or surround on the sides and above, through which an audience views the acting area.

festoon to drape by threading a cable through loops vertically sewn onto the backside of a cloth. By fixing this cable to the base of the cloth it can be raised by pulling up the cable from the top, thus festooning a cloth into swags.

fitch a brush for lining or painting in moulding lines, panelling, shading, shadowing or for all thin lines. A flat bristle brush cut in a wedge shape.

fit-up the installation of lighting, technical equipment and scenery on the stage.

flame proofing a liquid chemical solution applied to soft scenery, drapes, cloths and some soft props to make them non-flammable.

flat a standard scenic unit of either solid wood, or canvas and wood stretcher.

flies the area above the acting area for suspended scenery and lighting.

floorcloth a heavy canvas cloth with painted design used for covering the floor of an acting area.

flown any set or lighting suspended that is lowered and raised.

fly the process of bringing in and out what is suspended from the flies.

fly floor the gallery from which all flying is operated.

fly rail a handrail to the side of the stage where throw-lines are attached.

footlights a set of lanterns set on floor level along the down-stage edge that project up and back onto the actors.

fore and aft the measuring in direction of up-stage to down-stage, not its width.

fore-stage the acting area down-stage of a house curtain, tab or safety curtain.

fourth wall the imaginary wall between the audience and the acting space.

French brace a hinged support attached to the backside of scenery that opens out to create a brace.

French flat a wood-framed cloth with door, window or fireplace opening.

front cloth the designed drop or curtain placed between the audience and acting area.

front tab the black or house curtain masking the acting area from the audience.

gauze or scrim a loosely woven cloth that can be painted on. May serve as a softening when down-stage of a cyclorama. With lighting effects it can be made to appear solid, translucent or near-transparent.

get-in or get-out the process of installation or dismantling of lighting, equipment and scenery prior to and at the end of a production on-stage.

gobo a screen or metal cut-out placed in front of a light to create an effect on-stage.

grid the metal bar structure suspended below a ceiling for the fixing onto of lights and scenic units.

gridded raised scenery or unit to its limit of travel of the flying lines.

groundrow a low vertical strip of scenery set on floor level in an up-stage position across its width. May be designed as a cut-out.

ground plan the drawing depicting the view of the acting area seen from above.

header (1) A vertical strip hard or soft, hung with its base edge level with the top of the proscenium, running across the stage width, creating the first border. (2) The top to a scenic vertical, positioned to meet up with these verticals.

hemp-line the manhandled rope as part of the counterweight system.

house in reference to the auditorium.

house curtain the theatre's curtain or tab acting as the fourth wall.

inset a small scene set within a larger scene.

iron the fireproof curtain, usually solid, that acts as a seal between the stage and the auditorium.

kill to strike a set of furnishings and properties.

ladder framework for lights, can not be climbed.

laying-in brush a wide flat brush for applying base colours or a primer.

lead the principal part in a play.

leg cloth suspended vertically, acts as masking along with borders, running in sequence up-stage.

levels raised platforms above the stage.

line three cables attached to the bar leading up into the grid, named short, centre, long.

line-set term used to indicate a bar, often with accompanying number. As in LS #1.

mark out taping onto the rehearsal floor of the ground plan details to set and furniture placement.

masking hiding from view the areas outside the design and its acting area.

off-stage the area out of sight to the audience, beyond a set design and its acting area.

OP or **opposite prompt** the stage-right-hand side.

paint frame a wood framework to which cloths are attached for painting. The frame may track vertically through an aperture in the floor to below, or a bridge may elevate to help the painters move up and down.

perch a lighting position on the upstage side of the proscenium.

periactus a prism-shaped piece of scenery, trucked so as to offer three sides for design.

pin-hinge a hinge with removable pin, used to assemble flats and join units of scenery.

pipes a North American term for bars.

plate a triangular plywood piece attached to flats to reinforce the corners.

plot a listing of preparations and actions, used by workshop departments.

portal an opening through which the audience view the scene or acting area, having sides and a top. The design may involve several portal openings.

practical a prop or light fitting that is handled and used by an actor.

preset the set, furnishing, properties and all practicals in their position ready for the scene or act.

priming the first and base coat of paint, a mixture of whiting and size.

production manager organizes and schedules all the production technical preparations, which includes responsibility to production budget.

profile a shaped piece added to scenery to break up the straight edge.

prompt corner the stage-right offstage corner set up with desk and console for the stage manager to run the show.

properties or props all furnishings, set-dressing articles used in performance by actors.

PS or **prompt side** stage-left of the acting area.

pyrotechnics chemical effects used to produce specials in lighting or sound.

quick change room a suitable off-stage position for flats or curtain masking to enable an actor to quickly change costume.

rails the horizontal battens on the back of flats.

rake an ever-increasing slope to the stage as you travel up-stage. Also of inclined or ramped rostrum.

ramp a sloped level joining a level to a platform.

repertoire an organization having to alternate two or more productions over the course of a week.

repertory an organization that has the production run a limited length of time, one production is in rehearsal while another is on-stage running.

returns (1) Flats used either side of the stage joined to tormentors or legs. (2) That which is added to flats with windows, doorways, openings to give a flat the illusion of thickness.

reveal the thickness inherent to flats, detailing on windows and architecture at a right angle to the face of the flat.

revolve at a central position to the stage is a pivot for a circular turntable. A revolving stage.

risers the vertical planes of a step.

road on tour.

rostrum a platform level constructed to dismantle with sometimes a hinged framework so to store or tour.

runners a pair of curtains tracked horizontally to form a centre closure.

sandwich batten two battens with the cloth between.

scenographer a term for designer of scenery, where it is appreciated that the work provides an environment as an integral part of the production.

scrim *see* gauze

set to prepare or arrange a scene, or a call to set up.

setting line a line running parallel to the down-stage edge, positioned up-stage of the house curtain, from which all scenery is measured. Shown on the ground plan.

sightlines the eye view from the audience positioned in seats at the extreme points within a theatre's auditorium. This includes balcony and gallery back rows, and the pit front seats left and right.

sill or **sill iron** the flat steel bar spanning the foot of a door or arch, adding strength to the flat.

single purchase a counterweight system that has the cradle travel the same distance as the fly bars. The full height of the side wall is occupied with this system.

sky cloth a cyclorama.

SM stage manager.

snap line a line created by pulling taut a chalked string and snapping onto its surface.

spot line a rope or line dropped from the grid to suspend something in an exact special position.

stage cloth *see* floorcloth.

stage manager in overall control of the performance, calls actors to rehearsal, notes all rehearsal needs, works the running of the show through called cues that co-ordinate actors and technicians. Responsibility delegated to DSM and ASM.

stiles the outside frame of a flat. Also the verticals of a door frame, with one stile having hinging.

standing scenery not moved or altered in its position during a performance.

stipple to create plaster effects on a flat surface, the brush or sponge squeezed out of the required colour is dabbed onto the surface.

strike to remove scenery, props, furnishings in all or in part.

stringer the side walls of a stair unit to which the treads and risers are attached.

tab theatre curtain or house curtain. The original drew upwards and outwards.

tab-track the metal mechanics for attaching curtains which traverse the stage.

tallescope a vertical extendible ladder with an adjustable wheelbase, usually with outriggers for safety.

teaser a short masking drop flown in to hide scenery or other equipment.

tech technical rehearsal with all specials, changes of scenery rehearsed in relation to the whole play.

technical director co-ordinates and budgets the works of all departments.

three-fold flats hinged to fold, comprised of three units.

throwline or **lashline** the rope that temporarily secures two flats together through cleats and a slip knot.

toggle or **bar** the cross-piece in a flat frame.

tormentor narrow flats or legs positioned adjacent to and at right-angles to the up-stage side of the proscenium that stop at the setting line or false proscenium.

trap the opening to beneath stage, with steps or ladder for access. Traps lead to the under-stage, its passageways and cross-overs.

traverse a curtain that travels on a track.

treads the horizontal plane of a step or stair.

trim the height above stage level of a piece of scenery, masking, or lighting bar (North American term). The equivalent of Dead.

truck or **wagon** a mobile platform or rostrum.

up-stage the area away from the audience, towards the back.

wagon see truck.

wings (1) The areas to the sides of the acting area. (2) The scenery that stands where the acting area meets with the technical offstage areas.

wipe track a single curtain on a track, moved across the stage rather than being in two parts.

BIBLIOGRAPHY

Chaet, B., *The Art of Drawing* (Holt, Reinhart, Winston, 1970)

Griffiths, T.R., *Staging Handbook* (Phaidon, 1998)

Guthrie, T., *A Life in the Theatre* (Columbus Books Ltd, 1987)

Holt, M., *Stage Design and Properties* (Phaidon, 1988)

Melvill, H., *Designing and Painting Scenery for the Theatre* (Art Trade Press, 1948)

Reekie, F., *Reekie's Architectural Drawing* (Arnold, Hodder Headline Group, 1995)

Reid, F., *Designing for the Theatre* (A & C Black, 1996)

Reid, F., *The Staging Handbook* (A & C Black, 1995)

Sargent, W., *The Enjoyment and Use of Colour* (Dover NYC, 1964)

Southern, R., *Proscenium and Sight-Lines* (Faber & Faber, 1964)

Stewart, D.H., *Stagecraft* (Sir Isaac Pitman & Sons, 1949)

Thomas, T., *Create Your Own Stage Sets* (A & C Black, 1985)

Warre, Michael, *Designing and Making Stage Scenery* (Studio Vista, 1968)

INDEX

INDEX